ROAD TO HEAVEN

ROAD TO HEAVEN

ENCOUNTERS
WITH
CHINESE
HERMITS

BILL PORTER

Photographs by
Steven R. Johnson
and the author

Mercury House
San Francisco

Published in the United States by
Mercury House
San Francisco, California

United States Constitution, First Amendment: Congress shall make no law respecting an establishment of religion, or prohibiting the free exercise thereof; or abridging the freedom of speech, or of the press; or the right of the people peaceably to assemble, and to petition the Government for a redress of grievances.

Mercury House and colophon are registered trademarks
of Mercury House, Incorporated

Frontispiece: Bill Porter (second from left) and Steven R. Johnson (third from left) search for hermits in the Chungnan Mountains with a local guide (left) and Buddhist monk K'uan-ming (right).

Front cover photo and photos on pages 38, 81, 93, 110, 161, 171, 185, and 209 by the author.
Photos on pages 22, 30, and 203 from the collection of the National Palace Museum, Taipei, Taiwan, Republic of China.
All other photos by Steven R. Johnson.

Printed on acid-free paper
Manufactured in the United States of America

Library of Congress Cataloging-in-Publication Data
Porter, Bill, 1943–
  Road to heaven : encounters with Chinese hermits / by Bill Porter :
photographs by Steven R. Johnson and the author.
    p. cm.
  ISBN 1-56279-041-2
  1. Recluses—China.   2. Priests, Buddhist—China.   3. Taoists—China.
I. Johnson, Steven R.   II. Title.
CT9990.P67   1993
299′.51′0922—dc20
                                                              92-42339
                                                              CIP

5 4 3 2 1

for those who walk
the path of solitude

Contents

Chinese Dynasties and Republics

Hsia   2205–1766 B.C.
Shang   1766–1122 B.C.
Chou   1122–221 B.C.
Ch'in   221–206 B.C.
Han   206 B.C.–A.D. 221
THREE KINGDOMS PERIOD   221–265
Chin   265–420
NORTH-SOUTH DYNASTIES   420–589
Sui   589–618
T'ang   618–907
FIVE DYNASTIES   907–960
Sung   960–1278
Yuan   1278–1368
Ming   1368–1644
Ch'ing   1644–1911

Republic of China   1911–present (since 1949 limited to Taiwan)
People's Republic of China   1949–present

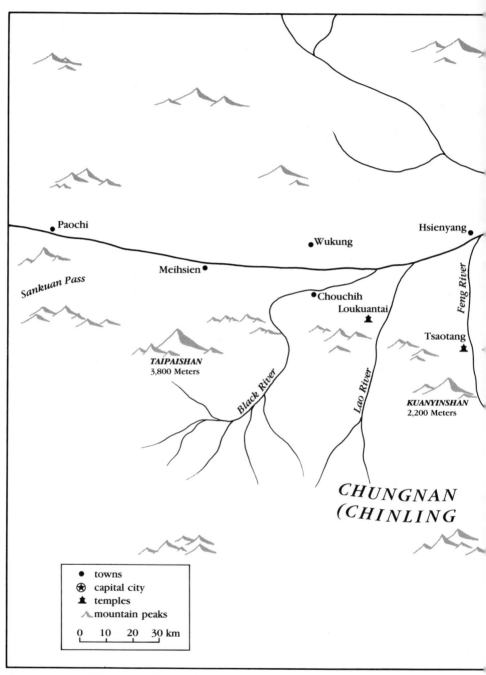

Sankuan Pass

Paochi

Meihsien

Wukung

Hsienyang

Chouchih
Loukuantai

Tsaotang

Feng River

TAIPAISHAN
3,800 Meters

Black River

Lao River

KUANYINSHAN
2,200 Meters

CHUNGNAN
(CHINLING

● towns
⊛ capital city
♨ temples
⌒ mountain peaks

0   10   20   30 km

Sian area and Chungnan Mountains.

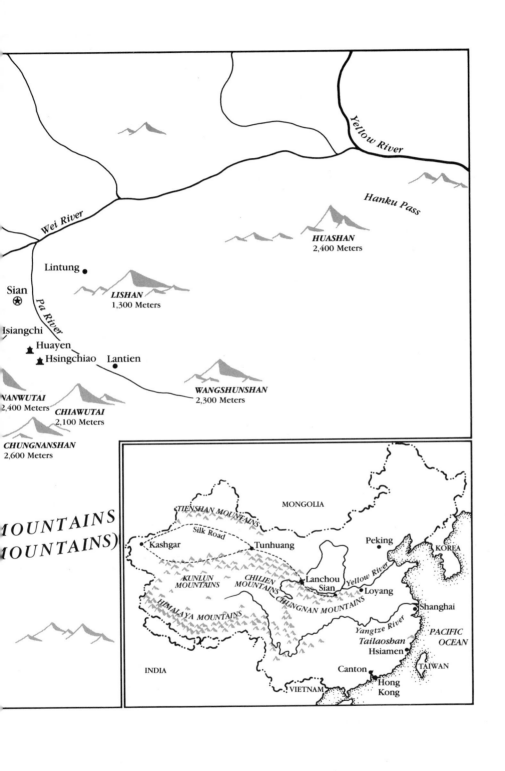

Yellow River

Hanku Pass

Wei River

HUASHAN
2,400 Meters

Lintung

Sian
⊛

Pa River

LISHAN
1,300 Meters

Isiangchi

Huayen

Hsingchiao   Lantien

WANGSHUNSHAN
2,300 Meters

NANWUTAI
2,400 Meters

CHIAWUTAI
2,100 Meters

CHUNGNANSHAN
2,600 Meters

MOUNTAINS
(OUNTAINS)

MONGOLIA

TIENSHAN MOUNTAINS

Silk Road

Kashgar   Tunhuang   Peking

KOREA

KUNLUN
MOUNTAINS

CHILIEN
MOUNTAINS

Lanchou
Sian   Yellow River   Loyang

CHUNGNAN MOUNTAINS

HIMALAYA MOUNTAINS

Shanghai

Yangtze River

PACIFIC
OCEAN

Tailaoshan

Hsiamen

INDIA

Canton   TAIWAN

VIETNAM   Hong
Kong

Chapter One

Hermit
Heaven

*T*hroughout Chinese history, there have always been people who preferred to spend their lives in the mountains, getting by on less, sleeping under thatch, wearing old clothes, working the higher slopes, not talking much, writing even less—maybe a few poems, a recipe or two. Out of touch with the times but not with the seasons, they cultivated roots of the spirit, trading flatland dust for mountain mist. Distant and insignificant, they were the most respected men and women in the world's oldest society.

No explanation has ever been offered or demanded for the admiration the Chinese have had for hermits. Hermits were simply there: beyond city walls, in the mountains, lone columns of smoke after a snowfall. As far back as records go, there were always hermits in China.

The Chinese say their history goes back five thousand years, back to the time of Huang-ti, the Yellow Emperor. Huang-ti was the earliest known leader of the confederation of tribes that established themselves along the Yellow River and that later called themselves Chinese. But it was from two hermits that Huang-ti learned how to conquer his enemies and how to prolong his life. And he reigned for a hundred

years, from 2700 to 2600 B.C., about the same time the first pyramids
were being built in Egypt.

After Huang-ti rode off on a dragon to join his fellow immortals,
leadership of China's nascent civilization passed through several hands
and, around 2300 B.C., into those of Yao. Two thousand years later,
Confucius praised Yao as the wisest of men because he passed over
members of his own family and chose a hermit as his successor.
Huang-fu Mi's third-century work, the *Kaoshihchuan* (Records of
High-Minded Men), recreates the occasion:

> Yao asked Hsu-yu to take over the kingdom. But Hsu-yu answered,
> "When the sun or moon is shining, what use is lighting a torch? When
> the rain is falling, what use is watering crops? You, sir, already rule the
> kingdom. Were I to replace you, it would be in name only. Name is
> the guest of reality, and I have no desire to be a guest. Even in a deep
> forest, the wren uses only one branch for its nest. Even beside a river,
> the tapir drinks only enough to fill its stomach. Go back, my lord. I
> have no need for a kingdom. If the cook fails to keep order in his
> kitchen, the shaman doesn't stop the ritual to take his place."

Instead of accepting Yao's offer, Hsu-yu washed out his ears in a
stream to rid them of any residue such talk might leave behind. But
Yao was determined to find a man of virtue and approached another
recluse, named Shun. Shun accepted Yao's offer, and eventually he
too looked for a hermit to succeed him. Again, the *Kaoshihchuan*
records the event:

> Shun tried to give the kingdom to a hermit named Shan-chuan. But
> Shan-chuan protested, "In former times, when Yao ruled the realm,
> people followed him without being told and praised him without being
> rewarded. The kingdom was at peace, and people were content. They
> didn't know hate or desire. Now you wear colored robes and confuse
> their eyes. You mix the five tones and confuse their ears. You play the
> music of Shao and stupefy their minds. This can only result in disorder,
> with which I want nothing to do. I have my place in the world. In win-
> ter, I wear skins. In summer, I wear hemp. In spring, I plough and
> plant and have enough to do. In fall, I harvest and gather and have

enough to eat. When the sun rises, I get up. When it sets, I rest. I'm free to do what I want in this world, and with this I'm content. What do I want with a kingdom? I'm afraid you've misjudged me." Shan-chuan disappeared into the mountains and was never heard from again.

Huang-fu Mi's versions of these stories are culled from the *Chuang-tzu* and other texts dating back to the fourth century B.C. or earlier. It seems that as soon as the Chinese began recording stories about their civilization's earliest leaders, they wrote stories about hermits. And for the past two thousand years they have repeated these hermit-ruler stories as ideals worth keeping in mind, if not emulating. Of course, crowded mountains won't do. But such stories weren't intended to create a society of hermits, assuming that were possible. They were aimed at those who exercised power. And their message was that transmission of power should be based on virtue and wisdom, not kinship.

These stories constitute China's earliest political criticism. But they aren't simply stories: there really were people who preferred the wilderness to civilization. This is the basis of the hermit tradition wherever it's found. But what distinguishes this tradition in China is the high status hermits have enjoyed in the society they supposedly left behind.

My own acquaintance with China's hermit tradition began in 1972, when I left the United States and moved to China's island-province of Taiwan, south of Shanghai, north of Hong Kong, off the coast of Fukien. Several days after I arrived, I began life in a Buddhist monastery: up before dawn to chant sutras, song of the bell at night, three vegetarian meals a day, a room, a bed, a mosquito net, no bill. When my legs got too sore or my mind too restless for the meditation cushion, I read.

In addition to Buddhist sutras, I read Confucian and Taoist texts that included dozens of stories about hermits in the hills of ancient China. They were my favorite stories. I could understand someone wanting nothing more than to live a simpler life: inside a cloud, under a pine tree, somewhere out of town, surviving on moonlight, taro, and hemp. Other than a mountain, they didn't need much: a little mud, some thatch, a patch of melons, a row of tea bushes, a trellis of chrysanthemums, a break in the weather. Since the Yellow Emperor's time, there must have been a million hermits in China. But reading about them made me wonder if they could have survived the twentieth century. Whenever I asked the monks in Taiwan, they assured me that China's hermits no longer existed. After a century of revolution, war, and oppression, how could they? Still, I wondered.

After three years, I traded monastic life for my own hermitage in the mountain village of Bamboo Lake overlooking the Taipei Basin, and I started translating the works of some of China's hermits of the past: Cold Mountain, Pickup and Big Shield, Stonehouse and Bodhidharma. Twelve years later, in the winter of 1987, the government on Taiwan lifted its ban on travel to the Chinese mainland, and people on the island began visiting relatives and friends they hadn't seen in forty years.

In the spring of 1989, I decided to join them, not to visit relatives, but to look for hermits. When a sympathetic sponsor agreed to finance an exploratory trip, I called up Steve Johnson in America. Two years earlier he had offered to join me as a photographer if such a trip should ever materialize. He hadn't changed his mind, and we agreed to meet two weeks later in Hong Kong. I got out my old forest service backpack and had new straps sewed on. I also began poring over maps, especially those showing population densities. I had no idea where we would find hermits but assumed that if any were left they would be in the mountains. But which mountains? And even if we happened to find the right mountain, how would we find the right trail, much less the right hut? And would they welcome visitors, especially a couple of foreigners brandishing a tape recorder and a camera? And would the authorities try to stop us? Lots of questions. No answers.

In traditional China, the hermit population rose and fell with changes in the wind that blew from the capital. I thought we might as well test the wind before heading into the mountains. After meeting in Hong Kong, Steve and I flew to Peking. We arrived on the last day of April, a few days after students in the city had launched their campaign to end political corruption and social oppression. A German friend in Peking offered to share his accommodations at the Summer Palace on the outskirts of the city, and we gladly accepted.

China keeps coming up with new ways of acquiring foreign exchange and had begun renting several courtyards of the former imperial resort to foreigners whose companies could afford it. Ironically, my friend was living in the same suite of rooms previously occupied by Chiang Ch'ing, Mao Tse-tung's widow and leader of the decade-long Cultural Revolution (1965–1976), which had supposedly rid China of its burdensome past, including its hermits.

After spending a night with Chiang Ch'ing's ghost, we visited Kuangchi Temple. The temple serves as the headquarters of the Buddhist Association of China, and I reasoned this would be a likely place to begin our search. I asked the organization's deputy director, Chou Shao-liang, if he knew where we might find a few hermits. Before he had time to recover from the question, the temple's abbot, Ching-hui, said he had heard reports of hermits living in the Chungnan Mountains near Sian.

I wasn't familiar with the Sian area and was about to ask for more information, but by then Chou had recovered. He said that there were no longer any hermits in China and that wandering around the Chungnan or any other mountains would not only be useless but dangerous. Instead, he suggested we visit one of the meditation centers that were once again active in China. He was kind enough to write down the locations of four such temples. I thanked him for his help, and we said good-bye. On the way out, I bowed to the abbot, whose faint smile I still remember.

Two days later, Steve and I returned from a visit to the Great Wall north of the city. We still had four hours before our train was due to leave for the ancient Buddhist center of Tatung northwest of Peking. But it was May 4, the anniversary of modern China's first student demonstrations seventy years earlier. The streets were thronged with demonstrators, and our taxi couldn't get within a mile of the train station. We had no choice but to get out, put on our backpacks, and begin making our way down Changan East Road. The police were standing in groups well away from the area, and no vehicles were being allowed anywhere near Tienanmen Square or the train station.

The demonstration must have included at least a hundred thousand students. But it was so orderly and festive it seemed more like a holiday parade than a political protest. Students in Tienanmen Square had organized themselves into units according to their academic department and school and were walking down Changan East Road holding up banners and chanting slogans. As they passed the train station and approached the Chinese Academy of Social Sciences, huge banners calling for democratic reforms were unfurled by people in the building. The students cheered. It was a lovely day. Over the sound of chants, applause, and occasional firecrackers, we could hear birds chirping and bicycle bells ringing. Everyone was smiling. We got drunk.

The next morning we woke up in pain in Tatung, and all I remember about the great buddha statues carved fifteen hundred years ago in the mountainside outside that most dismal of cities was how fortunate it was that someone had the foresight to plant lilac bushes near the caves. They were in bloom, and there was crawl space underneath.

The following day, we ventured into the countryside for the first time and visited Hengshan, northernmost of ancient China's five sacred mountains and home of hermits in the past. It was scenic enough, but we didn't see anything that looked like a hermit's hut.

The next day, we headed south for Wutaishan. Wutaishan was the ancient residence of Manjusri, Bodhisattva of Wisdom, and the northernmost of four mountains selected for special veneration by Buddhists in China. Situated in the middle of nowhere, it was, we thought, a likely place for hermits.

But it was not to be. There was hardly a tree in sight. I reasoned: no forests, no deadfall; no deadfall, no firewood; no firewood, no tea; no tea, no meditation; no meditation, no hermits. Though they might not have agreed with my reasoning, the abbots of the mountain's major monasteries agreed with my conclusion. Most of them were friends of the venerable Shou-yeh, former abbot of one of the biggest temples on the mountain and the monk with whom I had first "taken refuge" in the Triple Jewel of Buddhism in New York City. One after another, they assured me that nowadays all monks and nuns live in temples. As far as they knew, there were no hermits on Wutai-shan or on any other mountain in China.

Visiting one last temple, I stopped an old monk who was helping reconstruct one of the buildings damaged by the Red Guards during the Cultural Revolution. When I repeated my standard question, he said, "Of course there are still hermits in China." My heart stopped. Then he added, "But when you meet them, you won't know them. You won't find them, unless they want to be found." He laughed and returned to his work. I didn't know what to say, and that night I didn't fall asleep until quite late, wondering how we would find people who didn't want to be found and why I hadn't thought of this earlier.

The next day was Manjusri's Birthday, and I climbed the thousand steps to his shrine to offer my respects and ask his assistance in our search. Obviously, we were going to need help. Before the incense had burned down, we were aboard a bus and headed south. Again, my thoughts turned to what the old monk had said about hermits not wanting to be found. What exactly were we doing in China? Obviously, logic would have to go. We were on a mission.

The mission, however, took a break for tourism, as Steve and I contented ourselves with the sights of Sian, in whose environs eleven dynasties had built their capitals. After a few days of satisfying our historical curiosity, we were down to one last place to visit: Tsaotang Temple. This was where Kumarajiva stayed sixteen hundred years ago when he produced his transcendentally beautiful translations of Buddhist sutras. I couldn't pass up an opportunity to pay homage to this ancient master of an art of which I was, myself, a novice.

After a two-hour drive southwest of the city on muddy, rutted roads, we reached the temple's long red walls. They were surrounded by fields of wheat and looked as if they had been recently rebuilt. Despite the temple's ancient fame, it hardly looked worth the effort we had made to reach it. But once inside, I was surprised at the number of worshipers. The shrine hall was so packed, I barely found room to bow before the statues of Kumarajiva and Shakyamuni. As I was about to leave, an old monk appeared from out of the crowd and motioned me aside. He turned out to be the abbot, and the occasion that had attracted so many devotees was the Buddha's Birthday. How could I have forgotten?

After taking us on a tour of the temple grounds, the abbot led us into his private quarters. I told him we were looking for hermits. Meanwhile, several of his disciples had also crowded into the room. He looked at them, then at me. Finally, he said, "I don't know anything about hermits. But since you've come all this way, why don't you visit the stupa on the mountain you passed just before you turned off the main road? It contains the relics of Tao-hsuan, who certainly knew about the hermits of his day." The abbot escorted us to the gate, and we said good-bye many times.

We returned to the paved road and a few minutes later stopped at the foot of the peak mentioned by the abbot. After several false starts searching for the right path, we found an old man who agreed to serve as our guide. Halfway up, Steve and I began to wonder if the mountain had a top. The trail was so slippery from recent rains, we sometimes lost ground. An hour later, we finally reached the saddle.

Steve stopped to photograph the panorama, while I crawled up the final slope to the stupa. I circled the small brick structure three times and bowed in respect to this monk who had compiled the first chronicles of Buddhist worthies in China. Then I sat down and leaned against the front of the stupa. The view was one of endless serrated ridges, cloud-wrapped peaks, and turquoise streams. It looked like the perfect place for hermits. But even with the help of binoculars, I saw neither cave nor hut nor trail of steps nor wisp of smoke.

Disappointed, yet also rejuvenated by finally being in the mountains, I skidded back down to where Steve was resting. Our guide suggested that going down the trail on the back side of the mountain would be easier. That sounded fine to us, and down the back side we went.

After about ten minutes, the trail led past the mud walls of an old temple. We could hear voices from inside, and our guide knocked on the door. It opened, and five young monks ushered us through a courtyard and into a room that contained a table and five stools. We sat down, and they poured us cups of hot water and added something that looked and tasted like presweetened orange Kool-Aid.

Refreshed by this ancient ceremony of welcome, I asked our hosts the inevitable question: "Are there any hermits in these mountains?"

One of the monks answered, "Of course. Which hermits do you want to know about?" Over the next hour, we drank cup after cup of hot Kool-Aid and listened to a long list: some had been in the mountains for only one winter; others hadn't been down in forty years. We had found Hermit Heaven. Before leaving, I asked one of the monks the name of the mountains. He said, "These are the Chungnan Mountains. This is where monks and nuns come who are sincere about their practice."

In 1959, Arthur Wright ended his *Buddhism in Chinese History* (Stanford, Calif.: Stanford University Press) with this observation: "We are seeing, I believe, the last twilight of Chinese Buddhism as an organized religion" (p. 122). At the time, few people would have opposed such a pronouncement, and in the years that followed, Buddhism appeared to have been purged from the hearts and minds of the Chinese. Monasteries and nunneries that weren't burned or ransacked were turned into schools or factories. The few that remained were used to house the new monastic work crews, and most of their former residents were forced to return to the world of red dust. Over the past thirty years, observers both in and outside China have judged the campaign to root out the opiates and superstitions of the masses an overwhelming success. Most observers have written off Buddhism as a defunct religion. Whenever I raised the subject with John Blofeld, whose translations of the Zen teachings of Huang-po and Hui-hai were for many years my guide, he would sigh and suggest we talk about something else.

When I began thinking of visiting the Chinese mainland to see for myself, I concluded that if Buddhism were to survive in China, or anywhere else, it would depend not so much on monks and nuns living in temples as it would on them living in huts and caves. Looking back over the religion's twenty-five-hundred-year history, I couldn't think

Road to the Chungnan Mountains.

of any great master who had achieved his understanding of the Dharma without first undergoing a period of seclusion. When I finally decided to visit the mainland to see if Buddhism were still alive, I resolved to concentrate my efforts not on the monastic but on the hermit tradition.

At the time, I wasn't optimistic. Two weeks before I left, Ma Yingchou, the executive secretary of Taiwan's Mainland Affairs Committee, told me that the Communists had long since rid mainland China of hermits as well as of genuine monks or nuns. Who was I to argue? A month later, sitting in that small adobe temple with five young monks, looking through the doorway at the endless blue ridges of the Chungnan Mountains, drinking hot Kool-Aid, and writing down hermit addresses, I could only smile.

The next day, Steve and I left the Sian area and continued our odyssey across central China, climbing other mountains, talking to other hermits. Most of them were Buddhists, but many were Taoists; most were monks, but many were nuns; most were old, but many were young. They were all poor, but they had a way of smiling that made us feel we had met the happiest and wisest people in China.

One of the mountains we visited was Tailaoshan just inside the northwest tip of Fukien Province. A Buddhist layman we met on the trail led us to a cave where an eighty-five-year-old monk had been living for the past fifty years. In the course of our conversation, the monk asked me who this Chairman Mao was whom I kept mentioning. He said he had moved into the cave in 1939 after the spirits of the mountain appeared to him in a dream and asked him to become the mountain's protector. He hadn't been down the mountain since then. Disciples and local villagers brought him the few things he needed. And he didn't need much: flour, cooking oil, salt, and once every five years or so a new blanket or set of robes. His practice was the name of the Buddha: Amitabha, Buddha of the Infinite. After so many mountains and so many hermits, we were finally feeling at home with the infinite.

On our way down the mountain, we stopped to visit two hermits who had spent several decades in neighboring caves. As a parting gift,

Fifty years on Tailaoshan.

they gave us two kilos of Oriental Beauty from their own small tea or-chard. It was my favorite tea, and still is. No foreigners had ever visited their mountain, and they wanted to give us something special.

We continued down the trail to the village at the bottom of the mountain. The whole village was in an uproar. As soon as they saw us, they told us that the army had massacred thousands of protestors the previous night at Tienanmen Square. But they kept asking us what had really happened. No one believed what the government was tell-ing them, and they thought that foreigners must know more than they did. Those who had radios were keeping them tuned to the Chinese-language broadcasts of Voice of America or the BBC. We boarded a bus. It broke down. We flagged another bus, and eventually we reached Fuchou. In our hotel room, we watched the government replay of events that dominated every television newscast.

I thought back to a day we had spent in Wuhan. It was May 18, and our train must have been one of the last to arrive before students shut down the railway by blocking the Yangtze River Bridge. There are always so many people in Chinese cities, the crowds didn't strike us as unusual. We lined up to buy boat tickets to go down the river the next day and then went to find a hotel.

After checking in, we showered, washed our clothes, and went for our usual stroll in search of cold beer. We followed the flow of the crowd. Suddenly we were in the city square. A student passing a hat in front of us was collecting money to send fellow students to join their comrades at Tienanmen. I reached into my shirt pocket, intending to contribute 10 RMB, about two bucks. By mistake, I pulled out a hun-dred. It was too late to put the bill back. Stunned that anyone would give them so much money, the students carried me through the crowd and onto the steps of a monument where the demonstration leaders were addressing a crowd of several thousand people. They asked me to talk to them about democracy. I said a few words, certainly nothing memorable. They were so enthused by what they were doing they would have welcomed anyone, especially a foreigner, who agreed with their cause and could tell them so in Chinese. As I was stepping down to find Steve, I turned and wished them luck. One of them, who couldn't have been more than twenty, said, "We don't need luck. We're prepared to die." Sitting in Fuchou while the tanks rolled through Tienanmen, I wondered how many one-way tickets to Peking that 100 RMB had bought.

The following day, Steve and I took a bus to the port city of Hsiamen and boarded the next boat to Hong Kong. A few days later, we were back in Taiwan breathing a long sigh of relief but getting ready to return for a longer visit with hermits all over China. Potential sponsors, though, disappeared, and suddenly we were on our own. We thought about abandoning the project or waiting until political conditions improved. But we had found something we couldn't simply forget until it was more convenient or acceptable. In our minds we flipped a coin with two heads—and we went back six weeks later in early August. Obviously, we had to forget our plan to visit hermits throughout China. We had to restrict ourselves to what we could afford. After considering the possibilities, we chose Hermit Heaven.

Chapter Two

Mountains of the Moon

*W*hen I first heard about the Chungnan Mountains, I had no idea of their location or significance. In Peking, we were told they were near Sian and that was all. When we failed to find hermits on Hengshan or Wutaishan on our initial foray into the mountains, Steve and I boarded a train and headed south. We ended up sharing a compartment with two Sian businessmen. One of them had heard of Chungnanshan, that it was somewhere south of Sian, but that was all he knew. In Chinese, nouns aren't inflected and, hence, don't distinguish between plural and singular, so I still didn't know if *Chungnanshan* referred to one mountain or a range of mountains. A few days later, I found out it refers to both. Back in Taiwan, I learned it refers to more than mountains.

In modern times, the Chungnan Mountains include only the northernmost east-west ridges of a much larger range called the Chinling, or Range of Ch'in. The term *Chinling* came into use about two thousand years ago, sometime after the ancient state of Ch'in unified China from its ancestral base in the Wei River plain north of this range.

Nowadays, geographers, meteorologists, naturalists, and historians refer to the Chinling as the line that divides north and south China. Ever since it was uplifted a million years ago, the range has had a major influence on patterns of temperature and precipitation in China, blocking cold air from moving south in winter and preventing moist air from moving north in summer. Wheat, millet, and corn are the main crops north of the range. South of the range, it's rice.

The Chinling also forms the major watershed of China's two greatest rivers. The streams on its northern slopes flow into the Wei, the principal tributary of the Yellow River; and the streams on its southern slopes flow into the Han, the principal tributary of the Yangtze. In ancient times, when there was a drought, this was where officials came to pray for rain.

But a thousand years before the term *Chinling* came into use, the Chinese referred to the whole range as *Chungnanshan,* and sometimes they shortened this to *Nanshan.* The *Shihching,* or Book of Songs, mentions them in poems composed at least three thousand years ago:

> *what's on Chungnan*
> *catalpas and plum trees . . .*
>
> *what's on Chungnan*
> *rock spires and meadows . . .*

Now people apply the term *Chungnanshan* to the 2,600-meter peak forty kilometers south of Sian as well as to the adjacent mountains a hundred kilometers to the east and west. But three thousand years ago, *Chungnanshan* referred to all the mountains from the south shore of the Yellow River's Sanmen Gorge in Honan Province westward along the Wei River to the river's source on Wushushan, or Black Rat Mountain, in Kansu Province, a distance of 800 kilometers.

In China's more distant mythological past, *Chungnanshan* had an even wider application that went far beyond Black Rat Mountain. This greater range included the Kunlun as well as the Chungnan mountains and extended somewhat beyond K2 on China's current border with Pakistan, a distance of 3,500 kilometers.

In explaining the more limited application of *Chungnanshan,* early Chinese historians noted that *chung* means "end," *nan* means "south," and *shan* means "mountain" or "mountains." Thus, *Chungnanshan* was said to refer to the eastern end of the mountains that bordered the southern branch of the Silk Road. This explanation made sense of the component words, though it was, in fact, fortuitous and did nothing to explain the special significance these mountains had for the earliest Chinese, who viewed their peaks and valleys as the home of the most powerful heavenly and earthly spirits.

A more intriguing explanation is offered by Taiwan linguist Tu Er-wei, who contends that Chungnan and Kunlun are cognates, both stemming from a common word meaning "mountains of the moon." In his *Kunlun Wenhua yu Puszu Kuannien* (Kunlun Culture and the Concept of Immortality), Professor Tu explains that the Kunlun-Chungnan range represented the mythological focus of China's earliest religion, a religion that bridged the dark river between life and death by means of the concept of immortality as manifested by the waning and waxing of the moon. And since the moon goddess lived in the Kunlun-Chungnan range, this is where certain individuals came to gain access to the moon's divinity and the root of its powers.

They weren't ordinary members of society. Nor did they enter the mountains as ordinary people might. They walked the Walk of Yu, dragging one foot, as a wounded animal might, to elicit the pity of mountain spirits. Like Yu the Great, after whom this technique was named, they were shamans. And the Kunlun-Chungnan range was their earliest known home.

In his article on shamanism in the *Encyclopedia of Religion* (New York: Macmillan, 1987), Mircea Eliade notes that "throughout the immense area comprising the central and northern regions of Asia, the magico-religious life of society centers on the shaman" (vol. 13, p. 202). Eliade says that in such societies the ecstatic state is considered the ultimate religious experience, and the shaman is its master. In ecstatic trance, the shaman leaves his body, passes through a series of heavens, and communicates with all manner of spirits, seeking and gaining knowledge for the welfare of his community. By providing a link with the spiritual world and bringing back knowledge gained there, he defends his society against darkness. But at the same time, he lives apart from the society he protects.

A person called to be a shaman, according to Eliade, "seeks solitude, becomes absent-minded, loves to roam in the woods or unfrequented places, has visions, and sings in his sleep" (ibid.). Were it not for the ecstatic trance that initiates the novice shaman, this description could just as easily apply to someone following the hermit tradition. And in ancient China, the two were closely connected.

In tracing their connection, the earliest and most important text is one that describes how Ch'i, shaman emperor of the Hsia dynasty, entered the Chungnan-Kunlun range, flew off on a pair of dragons, and received from heaven the elegaic forms of verse used by later shaman-poets in such works as the *Chutzu,* or Songs of Ch'u.

Ch'i was the successor of another shaman, Yu the Great. When Yu founded the Hsia dynasty around 2200 B.C., he ordered his officials to compile a guide to the realm. The result was the *Shanhaiching* (Guide to Mountains and Seas), to which later emperors added as their knowledge of the realm's mysteries increased. Scholars doubt the book's antiquity and are unwilling to date any of its sections earlier than the fourth century B.C. But regardless of what scholars think about the book's date or its veracity, this geography of the spirit is a mine of shamanistic lore that must have been shared knowledge long before it was written down.

The book's chapter on western mountains begins with those south of Sanmen Gorge and continues along the Chungnan and Kunlun mountains all the way to K2 and beyond. Among their magical peaks are the earthly capital of Ti (the highest of heavenly spirits) and the home of Hsi-wang-mu (goddess of the moon and dispenser of the elixir of immortality). There are also mountains where shamans collect ingredients for their own elixirs and fly up to heaven, where people who die early live 800 years and meanwhile enjoy whatever they desire, where the sun and moon sleep, where anything is possible, and where creatures live that are too strange to believe but not to describe.

Recent archaeological excavations provide additional evidence suggesting shamanism was far more important than previously realized and that the foothills and plains north of the Chungnan Mountains were its earliest home in China. Archaeologist Chang Kwang-chih has called the shamanistic connection the most important aspect of early Chinese civilization. Chang notes, though, that shamans often needed a little help to communicate with the spiritual realm. Sex and alcohol were important and so were drugs.

In a neolithic village south of Lanchou and not far from Black Rat Mountain, archaeologists have found a clay pot containing carbonized buds of cultivated hemp, or *Cannabis sativa.* Paleobotanist Li Hui-lin thinks that the cultivation of this plant first occurred in this area, where it was used both as a textile fiber and as a drug. According to Li in *The Origins of Chinese Civilization,* edited by David N. Keightley (Berkeley: University of California Press, 1983), "Nomad tribes in the north, practitioners of shamanism, apparently used the plant as a drug and carried it west to central and western Asia and India, where it was used primarily as a hallucinogen and not as a textile fiber" (pp. 31–32). A quatrain from the "Greater Lord of Long Life" in the *Chutzu* makes clear the plant's significance to China's early shamans:

> *first a* yin *then a* yang
> *no one knows what I do*
> *jade buds of holy hemp*
> *for the one who lives apart*

The site where the hemp was found has been given a radiocarbon date of more than five thousand years ago. At the same site, archaeologists also found a bronze knife apparently used in sacrificial rituals. It not only constitutes the earliest bronze artifact found to date in China but also suggests that shamanism was sufficiently important to demand special materials unavailable for other, more profane, uses.

An even more important discovery regarding the development of shamanism in China was also made near the other end of the Chungnan Mountains. Among the artifacts uncovered at the neolithic settlement of Panpo, six kilometers east of Sian, are China's earliest form of writing as well as its earliest examples of shamanistic art: a shaman's fish-spirit mask and what appears to be an early form of the paired dragons used by Chinese shamans to aid them in their heavenly journeys.

The site at Panpo was occupied fairly continuously throughout the fifth millennium B.C., or seven thousand years ago, and it constitutes one of the best examples of China's Yangshao culture, which was followed by the Lungshan culture of the third millennium B.C. When Yu the Great founded the Hsia dynasty near the end of the third millennium, it could only have been on the basis of these Yangshao-Lungshan cultures that he and his ministers compiled the *Shanhai-ching,* the shaman's guide to the sacred world. Although the remains found at Panpo and other Yangshao-Lungshan sites are little more than suggestive, they at least permit us to conclude that no later than the fifth millennium B.C. someone was leaving this earthly realm to communicate with the world of spirits and was doing so near the Chungnan Mountains.

So how did shamans become hermits? Up until the end of the third millennium B.C., shamans occupied important positions in China's neolithic cultures. But the appearance of urbanization and social stratification that characterized the first dynastic states in the third and second millennia B.C. created a crisis for such individuals. The increasing bureaucratization of the decision-making process that accompanied these developments placed shamans under increasing suspicion. In *The World of Thought in Ancient China* (Cambridge: Harvard University Press, 1985), Benjamin Schwartz summarizes the ambiguous role of the shaman in a neolithic society evolving into a high civilization:

> Mircea Eliade defines the shaman in terms of his or her power to release his soul from his bodily frame in order to communicate directly with divine powers through ecstatic experience. The shaman may wander in the realm of the spirits or he may by trancelike procedures undergo possession by the spirits. Maspero contends, correctly, I believe, that in the long run shamanism was not compatible with the emerging religion of the state in China. This religion could not regard with favor a form of individual religious power that by claiming direct access to the divine

A hermit's hut. Painting by Lu Hung, eighth century. First in a series of ten paintings of the artist's hermitage on Sungshan, the easternmost spur of the Chungnan Mountains. Collection of the National Palace Museum, Taipei, Taiwan, Republic of China.

through ecstatic experience presumed to bypass the officially sanctioned ritual channels for communicating with divine spirits. (P. 36)

The shaman's influence was eclipsed by that of the bureaucrat. By analyzing oracle bone inscriptions of the second millennium B.C., Tung Tso-pin has shown that there was a steadily diminishing reliance on diviners and a gradual disappearance of sacrifice to nature deities and mythic ancestors (*Talu Tsachih,* vol. 6, pp. 1–6). The ritual of spiritual communication became so stylized that the drugged wine once drunk by the shaman was spit out by his bureaucratic successor. Such institutionalization doomed shamanism at court, where it was replaced by ritual behavior that was considered efficacious in itself yet cut adrift from its shamanistic roots.

With the advent of civilization, shamans became associated with mountains rather than urban centers. The *Shanhaiching* gives us the names of some of these shamans, the most prominent of whom lived in the Chungnan-Kunlun range. And thus began the hermit tradition that has lasted to this day.

It has lasted because the Chinese have always esteemed the past, and hermits preserved the most essential element of that past—its spiritual tradition. With the advent of civilization, this tradition was neither lost nor forgotten. Just the opposite. In China, hermits have remained the most esteemed of persons, because hermits are sages. They can see that to which others are blind and hear that to which others are deaf.

When emperors, kings, clan chiefs, leaders of early Chinese culture needed to get in touch with natural forces, the gods outside the city wall and inside the human heart, they turned to hermits. Hermits could talk to heaven. They knew its signs, they spoke its language. Hermits were shamans and diviners, herbalists and doctors, adepts of the occult and the manifest. Their world was far bigger than the walled-in world of the city. Detached from values imposed by whim or custom, hermits have remained an integral part of Chinese society because of their commitment to their culture's own most ancient values. If nothing else, they represent its mythic past, and that past is nowhere more apparent than in the many faces of the Mountains of the Moon—whether called Kunlunshan, Chungnanshan, or simply Nanshan—to which this prayer in the *Shihching* (Book of Songs) bows its head:

> *the smile of the moon*
> *the glory of the sun*
> *the age of Nanshan*
> *by change untouched*

Chapter Three

If the
World Is
Muddy

Although the hermit tradition was an integral part of Chinese society, it wasn't until the end of the third century A.D. that Chinese officialdom bothered to address the contribution of hermits. The authors of the *Houhanshu* (History of the Later Han Dynasty) begin a special section on hermits with this observation:

> Some retired to achieve their ideals; some bowed out to maintain their principles; some chose quiet to still their passions; some chose escape to preserve their lives; some to shame others into changing their ways; some to cleanse themselves.

The authors go on to note that despite such differences these individuals all shared the same unchanging goal: to follow the Tao. And for them, the Tao led out of town. Even though Confucius agreed, "The Tao no longer prevails," he stayed in town, because he thought it was his duty as a man who revered the Tao to convince those in power that anyone who ruled according to the Tao would become a pole star around which the world would move in harmony.

Not everyone was so optimistic. Feigning madness to protect him-

self against the insanity of the times, the Madman of Ch'u walked past
Confucius singing:

> *Phoenix, oh Phoenix, virtue has faded*
> *the past is immune to instruction*
> *the future is yet to see*
> *give it up, give it up*
> *to serve now is fraught with danger*
> (Confucius, *Analects,* chap. 18)

For some, following the Tao meant a life of seclusion. For others,
it meant a life of public service. Regardless of the choice a given individual may have made, throughout Chinese history there was a
never-ending dialectic between these two alternatives. In the *Chutzu,*
"The Fisherman" continues the dialogue:

> *when Ch'u Yuan was banished*
> *he wandered along rivers*
> *he sang on their banks*
> *weak and forlorn*
> *till a fisherman asked*
> *aren't you the Lord of the Gorges*
> *what fate has brought you to this*
> *and Ch'u Yuan answered*
> *the world is muddy*
> *I alone am clean*
> *everyone is drunk*
> *I alone am sober*
> *and so they sent me away*
> *and the fisherman said*
> *a sage isn't bothered by others*
> *he can change with the times*
> *if the world is muddy*

splash in the mire
if everyone is drunk
drink up the dregs
why get banished
for deep thought and purpose
and Ch'u Yuan said he had heard
when you clean your hair
you should dust off your hat
when you take a bath
you should shake out your robe
why should I let something so pure
be ruined and wronged by others
I'd rather jump into the Hsiang
and be buried in a fish's gut
than let something so white
be stained by common dirt
the fisherman smiled and rowed away singing
when the Tsanglang is clear I wash my hat
when the Tsanglang is muddy I wash my feet
and once gone he was heard from no more

Ch'u Yuan was China's first great poet. He was also a shaman and served in that capacity around 300 B.C. at the court of Ch'u, near which the Tsanglang River flowed. Critical of his ruler's faults and slandered by rivals, he was banished to the marshes south of the Yangtze, where the fisherman met him wandering along the banks of the Hsiang River. Disappointed by his ruler's blindness and barred from further service, Ch'u Yuan's course should have been clear, and near the end of "Encountering Sorrow," he wrote:

how can I live with cold-hearted people
oh let me leave them behind
toward Kunlun I turn my path
the long ever-winding road

But Ch'u Yuan couldn't bring himself to become a hermit. He never reached the Kunlun-Chungnan range. He ignored the fisherman's advice and jumped into the Milo River, just east of where it enters the Hsiang.

The Chinese still row their dragon boats on the fifth day of the fifth lunar month to save Ch'u Yuan. And people throw balls of rice wrapped in bamboo leaves into the water to keep the fish and water-dragons distracted long enough for the boats to reach him. But despite all this effort, the poet drowns every year, and the waters of China only become muddier.

The conflict between virtue and politics was at the heart of the hermit tradition. If Ch'u Yuan found it difficult to resolve the two to his satisfaction, he wasn't alone. Eight hundred years before Ch'u Yuan jumped into the Milo River, two brothers confronted the same problem. Their names were Po-yi and Shu-ch'i, and such was their adherence to principle that when they learned that the founder of the new Chou dynasty had revolted against his own ruler and launched a military campaign without properly mourning his father, they shook their sleeves in disgust and moved to Shouyangshan. Shouyangshan was on the north shore of the Yellow River across from the eastern end of the Chungnan Mountains and not far from where Shun (whom Emperor Yao chose to succeed him) had once lived in retirement before his elevation to the throne. Shun was known for the same virtues of filial piety and loyalty esteemed by Po-yi and Shu-ch'i. But unlike Shun, the brothers failed to meet a ruler who recognized their virtue. Meanwhile, they resolved to stop eating the produce of the kingdom and to subsist, instead, on a blameless diet of doe's milk and ferns. Eventually they starved to death. In their biography, Szu-ma Ch'ien says they often sang this song to take their minds off their hunger:

> *climb that west slope*
> *pick those ferns*
> *trading evil for evil*
> *don't they know is wrong*
> *the sage kings are gone*

where can we go
oh we're both finished
life doesn't last

In the *Analects,* Confucius comments, "Duke Ching of Ch'i had thousands of horses. But when he died, nobody found anything to praise. Po-yi and Shu-ch'i starved at the foot of Shouyang, yet people praise them to this day" (chap. 16). Mencius (c. 371–c. 289 B.C.) called Po-yi "the pure one among the sages." Yet in praising these brothers, Confucius and Mencius told their disciples that such behavior was overscrupulous and not worthy of emulation. Confucius and Mencius, no doubt, would have served.

Not all followers of the Tao, though, saw the choice between service and obscurity in such clear-cut terms. Two such men were Chang Liang and Chu-ko Liang.

Chang Liang was the descendant of a family that for generations had provided ministers to the state of Hann in what is now Honan Province. In 230 B.C., Hann was absorbed by the state of Ch'in in its advance to establish dominion over all of China. And Chang, being a filial son and a loyal subject, swore to avenge the honor of his family and state. But to make sure he lived long enough to achieve his goal, he first retired to the hills. And while he was living in retirement, he met an old man who put his humility to the test. The old man turned out to be a Taoist immortal who rewarded Chang with a copy of Lushang's long-lost *Art of War.* Chang proved an apt pupil, and when he finally came out of retirement, he helped Liu Pang overthrow the Ch'in and found the Han dynasty.

The new emperor expressed his gratitude to Chang by offering him any fief he desired, and Chang chose Liupei, on the southern side of the Chungnan Mountains. Chang then announced his intention to retire from worldly affairs, and he stopped eating grains and practiced breath control, hoping to make himself light enough to ascend to heaven, which he finally did in 187 B.C.

Earlier, when Chang Liang was still in hiding and studying the lessons of Lushang, the new Ch'in dynasty began recruiting scholars from all over China. The Ch'in administration, however, was known for its harshness, and four friends who refused to serve were Tung Yuan, Lu Li, Ch'i Li-chi, and Hsia Huang. These Four Worthies, as they became known, refused to compromise their principles, and they retired to Shangshan on the sunny side of the Chungnan Mountains, where they supported themselves by gathering medicinal plants. According to the *Hanshu* (History of the Han Dynasty), they often sang this song to amuse themselves:

> *forested mountains*
> *winding valleys*
> *bright purple mushrooms*
> *to keep away hunger*
> *with sages so distant*
> *where can we turn*
> *horses and carriages*
> *bring nothing but worries*
> *merchants and kings*
> *are no match for paupers*

Though they remained in seclusion, their names traveled far. The First Emperor tried to lure them out of the mountains, as did Liu Pang. Both failed. Later, when Liu Pang was about to replace the crown prince with the son of his favorite concubine, Empress Lu asked Chang Liang for help. And using Chang's advice, she convinced the Four Worthies that the crown prince was a man who honored wisdom and humility above wealth and power. They came to the capital and accompanied the crown prince to the palace. When Kao-tsu saw that the crown prince had managed to gain the respect of these men, he changed his mind about replacing him and told the Four Worthies to take good care of his son.

An even more famous example of a recluse who ended his years of seclusion to enter the service of a righteous lord was Chu-ko Liang, who was born in A.D. 181, just as rebellions were breaking out across the country. When he was still young, he moved to a village outside Chingchou in what is now Hupei Province to escape the troubled

The Four Worthies. Painting by Hsieh Shih-ch'en, sixteenth century. Collection of the National Palace Museum, Taipei, Taiwan, Republic of China.

times. And here he spent the next ten years living as a recluse and studying with another famous recluse, Szu-ma Hui.

During this chaotic period, the rulers of the Han dynasty lost control of the central government to a group of generals led by Ts'ao Ts'ao, and regional strongmen set up their own states. One such state was centered around Chingchou, where Ch'u Yuan had once served before his banishment. This was also where Liu Pei fled in A.D. 201 to escape Ts'ao Ts'ao. Liu Pei was a distant relative of the imperial family, and he had gathered an army to restore the dynasty to power. But he still lacked someone who could lay far-reaching plans.

When Liu Pei heard that Chu-ko Liang might be such a man, he resolved to see for himself. As sometimes happened even when prominent men called on hermits, Liu Pei had to visit Chu-ko Liang's thatched hut three times before he was received. When the two finally met, Liu Pei was so impressed with Chu-ko Liang's grasp of strategy, he begged him to end his seclusion and come to the aid of the country, and Chu-ko Liang agreed.

In the years that followed, Chu-ko Liang left no doubt that China had never seen a greater strategist. On one occasion, he drove off an army of two hundred thousand with a force of only two thousand. And rare is the Chinese who hasn't read about his exploits in *The Romance of the Three Kingdoms.* Chu-ko Liang finally died of illness in 234 during a military campaign in the foothills of the Chungnan Mountains west of Sian. The day he died, a shooting star fell near his encampment, and it was later incorporated into one of the walls of the shrine that still overlooks the valley where they both fell.

Before he died, Chu-ko Liang offered his son this advice on how to resolve the conflicting demands of seclusion and public service:

> The course of a gentleman is to cultivate his person through tranquillity and to nourish his virtue through honesty. Unless he is calm, his ideals cannot manifest themselves. Unless he is still, his influence cannot reach far. Learning requires tranquillity, and ability requires learning. If not through learning, he has no means to broaden himself. If not through ideals, he has no means to complete his learning. If he is dissolute, he cannot rouse his spirit. If he is rash, he cannot govern

his nature. While he is still young, he spurs himself on. While he still can, he completes his work. Decay seldom receives the world's sympathy. What can he accomplish, if he remains in seclusion?

And on this point has hinged the major difference among followers of the Tao: to serve or not to serve, to hide one's light or to let it shine forth—assuming, as Mathew Arnold once put it, that "one's light be not darkness." The difference has been not so much a matter of philosophy as of temperament and perception. The aim has remained the same: the application of the principles of the Tao to human affairs. This was true for Confucius, for Ch'u Yuan, for Po-yi and Shu-ch'i, as well as for Chang Liang, the Four Worthies, and Chu-ko Liang. While a period of relative seclusion was considered essential to understand these principles, and seclusion sometimes lasted a lifetime, the aim remained the establishment and extension of harmony in the world.

Seclusion and public service were seen as the dark and light of the moon, inseparable and complementary. Hermits and officials were often the same people at different times of their lives. And officials who never experienced tranquillity and concentration of spirit in pursuits other than fame or fortune were not esteemed in China. The Chinese have always looked to hermits as among their greatest social benefactors and have encouraged rather then discouraged their pursuit of the Tao, however unconventional and reclusive such pursuit might seem. Whether or not they have come out of retirement to serve, hermits have influenced the entire culture as springs of pure thinking and pure living that sooner or later find their way to town.

While China's first great poet buried himself in a fish's gut when he was exiled from court, the country's second great poet couldn't wait to quit his official post and retire to the countryside. In one of his "Drinking Poems," T'ao Yuan-ming provides a glimpse of the spirit that liberated China's followers of the Tao and that kept their minds, if not their bodies, free of city dust:

> *I built my hut beside a path*
> *but hear no cart or horse*

> *you ask how can this be*
> *a distant mind is a far-off place*
> *picking mums by the eastern fence*
> *I lose myself in the southern hills*
> *the mountain air the sunset light*
> *birds flying home together*
> *in this there is a truth*
> *to know but not to say*

The hermits of China have remained one of its best-kept secrets and represent much of what is most mysterious about this country. Where else is the wisdom of a civilization traced to mindlessness, as in this biographical sketch that begins the *Kaoshihchuan,* the earliest book about China's hermits:

Emperor Yao's teacher was Hsu-yu, and Hsu-yu's teacher was Nieh-ch'ueh. Nieh-ch'ueh's teacher was Wang-ni, and Wang-ni's teacher was P'i-yi. Nieh-ch'ueh once asked P'i-yi about the Way. P'i-yi said, "Straighten your body and concentrate your vision, and the harmony of Heaven will prevail. Collect your thoughts and focus your mind, and spirits will come down, virtue will adorn you, the Way will accompany you. You'll stare at things like a new-born calf without looking for reasons." But before P'i-yi had finished, Nieh-ch'ueh was asleep. P'i-yi laughed and walked away singing:

> *dry bones for a body*
> *cold ashes for a mind*
> *his wisdom simply true*
> *he doesn't ask for reasons*
> *vacuous and mindless*
> *not worth your time*
> *tell me his name*

Chapter Four

On the Trail of the Tao

*W*hen the Chinese began to put their understanding of the universe into words, the one word they all used was *tao,* a word that meant a road, a way, and, by extension, a way of life. But in the beginning, the Tao wasn't the province of travelers or philosophers but of tribal shamans concerned with the relationship between the living and the dead, a relationship that they saw more clearly reflected in the waning and waxing—the yin and yang—of the moon than anywhere else.

According to the linguistic and textual analyses of Tu Er-wei, the word *tao* originally referred to the phases of the moon. China's earliest Taoists were moon-faced shamans, men and women who used their power of soul flight to search for the secret of the moon's perpetual renewal, its immortality. As far as China's early shamans and their Taoist successors were concerned, the sun was a constant. In the world of change, the moon held all the secrets. To search for the secrets of the Tao was to search for the secrets of the moon. And to search for the secrets of the moon was to live where the moon's powers held sway, beyond the walls built to keep out change.

One day nearly five thousand years ago, the Yellow Emperor met one of these early Taoists, in the mountains of northwest China. His name was Kuang Ch'eng-tzu, and during the course of their meeting, Huang-ti asked Kuang the secret of immortality. Kuang's answer was recorded two thousand years later in the *Chuangtzu:*

> Let your mind be still and pure. If you want to live forever, don't exhaust your body or its vitality. Your eyes should see nothing. Your ears should hear nothing. Your mind should know nothing. Let your spirit take care of your body, and your body will last forever. Concentrate on the inside. Ignore the outside. Knowledge will only harm you. (Chap. 11)

From Kuang Ch'eng-tzu and others who lived on the fringes of China's early civilization, Huang-ti learned the secrets of Taoist cultivation. During his reign of a hundred years, Huang-ti in turn spread Taoist teachings across northern China and at the same time laid the basis for China's common cultural heritage. In early April, on the day set aside for visiting ancestral graves, high government officials still visit Huang-ti's grave in northwest China to pay their respects to the man considered the founder of Chinese culture as well as Taoism.

Although such an amorphous religion as Taoism can hardly be said to have had a founder, Huang-ti's name has been used both to indicate the religion's antiquity and to link its development with one of the culture's earliest heroes. But while Taoism may have been conceived in the womb of Huang-ti, it remained in embryonic form for another two thousand years, until Lao-tzu stopped long enough in the Chungnan Mountains to deliver the child into the hands of Yin Hsi.

When Szu-ma Ch'ien wrote his *Shihchi* (Historical Records) around 100 B.C. and Pan Ku compiled his *Hanshu* (History of the Han Dynasty) around A.D. 100, they applied the Taoist label to military strategists, political thinkers, literary figures, and philosophers of very different views. In the beginning, the Tao was big enough to include just about any view under heaven, and during this period of the Big Tao China's earliest historians put Lao-tzu at the head of the class.

As was the case with Huang-ti, Taoism's legendary progenitor, Lao-tzu was doubtlessly passing on wisdom expressed earlier by others. For example, Lao-tzu's approach is often summed up by the words *wu-wei,* "effortlessness." But two thousand years before, not long after

Huang-ti disappeared into the clouds, Emperor Shun was said to have exercised his rule over the tribes of northern China by merely facing south. To Lao-tzu, though, goes the credit of putting this wisdom into words, words that even Lao-tzu admitted could not express the mystery of mysteries that was the Tao. Of course, Taoists who trace their ancestry back to Lao-tzu say he taught more than effortlessness. He also taught the secrets of self-cultivation that have ever since been transmitted from master to disciple through oral instruction and texts too cryptic to understand without the help of a guide.

According to his earliest biographers, Lao-tzu was born old in 604 B.C. and served in the Eastern Chou capital of Loyang as curator of the Royal Archives. Among the areas in which Lao-tzu possessed uncommon knowledge was the realm of ritual, a not unusual specialization for someone whose spiritual ancestors were shamans. When he was eighty-eight, he was visited by the young Confucius, who came to Loyang from the state of Lu to increase his knowledge of the ceremonies of the ancients. In his *Shihchi*, Szu-ma Ch'ien recorded Lao-tzu's advice to his visitor:

> The ancients you admire have been in the ground a long time. Their bones have turned to dust. Only their words remain. Those among them who were wise rode in carriages when times were good and slipped quietly away when times were bad. I've heard that the clever merchant hides his wealth so his store looks empty and that the superior man acts dumb so he can avoid calling attention to himself. I advise you to get rid of your excessive pride and ambition. They won't do you any good. This is all I have to say to you.

Except for this story of his meeting with Confucius and its repetition in various forms in the *Chuangtzu* and other early Taoist texts, the only other information we have about Lao-tzu is the story of his disappearance beyond the Chungnan Mountains.

The transfer of the Chou capital east from the Wei River plain to the edge of the Yellow River plain marked the beginning of what historians call the Eastern Chou and the decline of the dynasty's power. Along with their declining power, Chou rulers also displayed

Statue of Lao-tzu near Loukuantai.

diminishing virtue, and a host of kingdoms, equally lacking in virtuous rulers, competed to establish a new hegemony. Not long after his meeting with Confucius, Lao-tzu decided to take his own advice and slipped quietly away, riding off on his blue ox.

Several days later, Lao-tzu reached Hanku Pass, where he was welcomed by Yin Hsi. Yin Hsi was also a follower of the Tao. Earlier, from his observatory in the Chungnan Mountains, he had seen a purple cloud moving across the sky from east to west and had deduced from his knowledge of heavenly signs that a sage would soon be passing through the area. He had subsequently arranged for his appointment as warden of the pass normally used by travelers coming from the east, and he recognized Lao-tzu as the sage he was waiting for. Following Lao-tzu's arrival, he resigned from his new post and invited the sage to accompany him to his observatory at Loukuantai. Although Loukuantai was 250 kilometers to the west, it was in the same direction as Lao-tzu was traveling, and the two men continued there together.

Nothing more is known about their meeting and journey, except that at the end of it, Lao-tzu delivered into Yin Hsi's hands the *Taoteching,* Taoism's earliest scripture and one yet to be surpassed for an explanation of the Tao. When I first began studying classical Chinese twenty years ago, this was among my favorite texts. And when I learned that it had been written in the Chungnan Mountains, I decided to follow its author's trail.

We hired a car and driver and began at the narrow defile of Hanku Pass, which cuts through the loess foothills between the Yellow River and the eastern end of the Chungnan Mountains near the town of Lingpao. There was only enough room for a cart—or an ox—and we had to use the new paved road several kilometers to the south. From Hanku Pass, we traced Lao-tzu's route westward past the towering summit of Huashan and the hot spring baths of Lishan and followed the sage out Sian's West Gate. After one police check, we turned southwest at Sanchiaochen.

Police in China are like trolls. The normal cost of a police check is anywhere from 20 to 100 RMB, or as much as twenty dollars, depending on which papers aren't in order and how much is needed to meet the monthly quota that guarantees policemen their elite life-style. Fortunately, all five sets of our driver's papers were in order.

After three more police checks, we reached the village of Mawangchen and took a road on the right. It led past a gate that enclosed several royal graves unearthed in 1955. This area was the location of Feng and Hao, the twin capitals of the Chou dynasty, until they were destroyed by invaders in the eighth century and replaced by Loyang. Two hundred years later, as Lao-tzu passed by their ruins on his way to Loukuantai, he must have been reminded of mankind's transient glory. In his notebook on the Tao, he wrote:

> *we can see the cost of desire*
> *the loss of what we keep*

A hand-written sign on the gate said, "Closed to the public. Access by special permission only." The gate wasn't locked, so we walked inside. There was no one around, but we had no trouble finding the building that enclosed the pit where archaeologists have left two chariots in situ. They were buried to serve Chou royalty in the afterlife. The door was locked, but through the window we could see their wheels and frames still in place along with the bones of six horses. We didn't see any sign of the drivers. Through the windows of two other buildings we saw nothing but empty display cases. I recalled the hundreds of pieces of smuggled Chou pottery I had seen a dozen years earlier in Taiwan as it passed through the hands of a well-connected friend on its way to foreign buyers. Pieces of intact three-thousand-year-old Chou pottery were going for as little as a hundred dollars. Unfortunately, those were my monastery days, and I didn't have a hundred dollars.

We left the buried ruins of Feng and Hao behind and continued heading west. At the town of Tawangchen, we turned south, stopped for another police check, and eventually reached the county seat of Huhsien. On a side street near the middle of town, we stopped at an exhibition hall. In 1958, the central government began encouraging farmers to take up arts and crafts. Since then, the farmers of Huhsien have become among the most famous painters in China. Whenever they're not busy with farm work, they pedal their bicycles to local centers where they're supplied with paper, brushes, poster paints, and a minimum of instruction.

Spring planting hadn't begun, and we met one of the artists inside the hall. His name was Lo Chih-chien, and he showed us his works. They impressed me, and I asked if he had ever painted the Chungnan Mountains. When he said he hadn't, I asked him to try. Four months later, a friend from Taiwan stopped in Huhsien and picked up the finished painting — a blue river flowing out of blue mountains watered by a blue sky.

After one last police check in Huhsien, we turned west and crossed the Lao River. Ten kilometers later, we left the main road for the nearby village of Tsuantsun and the site of Chungyang Temple, one of China's most famous Taoist centers of the past. It was built in the thirteenth century in honor of Wang Ch'ung-yang, founder of the Chuan Chen school of Taoism.

Not long after Wang became a soldier, he saw through life's illusions and moved to this area to practice Buddhist meditation. Several years later, wandering in the nearby Chungnan Mountains, he met the Taoist immortals Lu Tung-pin and Han Chung-li and received from them the secret oral teachings of Taoism. After this initiation, Wang spent seven years here, three of them living in a hole he called "the grave of a living corpse." In his writings, he combined elements of Zen Buddhism and Neo-Confucianism with the traditional Taoist emphasis on nurturing one's life force. Before his death in 1170, he succeeded in transmitting his understanding of the Tao to seven disciples in far-off Shantung Province, and four of them brought their master's mortal body back to the site of his former "grave."

In an extension of the Confucian custom of mourning one's parents, all four disciples built huts near the grave and remained in the area for three years before leaving to spread their master's teachings. One of the four, Ch'iu Ch'ang-ch'un, eventually succeeded in reaching the camp of Genghis Khan in Central Asia in 1222 and won from him a decree granting the school and its adherents special privileges in that part of northern China under Mongol control. Ever since then, the Chuan Chen school has been considered the principal keeper of the Taoist flame in China, adding monasticism to the traditional Taoist practices of alchemy, yoga, and meditation.

Soon after it was built, Chungyang Temple became what must have been the biggest religious complex ever constructed in China. It was funded by the Mongol royal family and housed ten thousand Taoist monks and nuns. During our visit, all we saw to suggest the temple's former glory was one teetering shrine hall and several dozen steles, or stone slabs, just inside the north wall. The steles all dated from the thirteenth century and included a portrait of Wang Ch'ung-yang as well as portraits of his seven disciples. Also on display was a stele with Wang's bold and fluid calligraphy as well as several others with examples of the Mongol script. Despite the presence of two old Taoist monks to take care of the shrine hall, the site was under government control, as were most religious sites of historical significance in China. The officials in charge reacted to our presence with suspicion, and as soon as we finished examining the steles, we left.

West of the temple, we turned south along a river. Village women were washing clothes and bed sheets on boulders along the bank. To the south, we could see the river's source on the nearby peaks of the Chungnan Mountains. After a short distance, we rejoined the main road and headed west again. After about fifteen kilometers, we stopped just short of the Tien River. Beyond its wide gravel bed rose the forested knoll of Loukuantai, home of the *Taoteching*.

In ancient times, rulers considered a knowledge of the Way of Heaven crucial to the conduct of state affairs. Battles were often decided by the weather; dynasties rose and fell on the tails of comets. Soon after the Chou dynasty was founded in the eleventh century B.C., King K'ang is said to have ordered an observatory established on this knoll, a long day's ride from the capitals of Feng and Hao. During the next century, King Mu visited the site and ordered construction of a shrine. The knoll later became known as Loukuantai, the Observation Tower, and its most famous observer was Yin Hsi, who led Lao-tzu here after their meeting at Hanku Pass.

Past the river, we turned and headed for the knoll. On the left, we passed a wall that enclosed the site of the former imperial shrines. In 219 B.C., eight hundred years after King Mu built the first shrine, the First Emperor of the Ch'in dynasty also built a shrine here, to Lao-tzu. A hundred years later, Emperor Wu of the Han dynasty followed suit. The site was also honored by other emperors. But none of the earlier shrines compared with the complex of over fifty structures that Kao-tsu built, soon after he founded the T'ang dynasty in A.D. 618.

Kao-tsu's family name was Li, the same as Lao-tzu's, and his ancestry was conveniently traced to that of the sage. Loukuantai subsequently became the royal family's ancestral shrine, and it was renamed Tsungshengkung, Temple of the Ancestral Sage. Today, nothing remains behind the new wall of gray brick except a number of steles recording Loukuantai's early history and an ancient gingko tree said to have been planted by Lao-tzu. Gingkos are extremely slow-growing, and this one is huge and still flourishing, despite losing its interior to fire.

After visiting Lao-tzu's gingko, we continued up the tree-lined road through a small village and then through an archway announcing Loukuantai Forest Park. On the right was a newly built and already deteriorating two-storey hotel. It was as deserted as the graveyard of steles we'd left on the road below. Past the hotel we entered the temple gate and stopped to register at the temple hostel. The cost for a bed was 10 RMB per night, two bucks.

Beyond the hostel was a dirt courtyard with another ancient gingko and a well, and behind the well was a hall that contained steles commemorating Loukuantai's periodic restorations. We followed a passageway through the hall to stone steps leading up the south slope of the knoll to the main shrine on top. This is where Lao-tzu is said to have taught Yin Hsi the lessons that made up the *Taoteching*. Just inside the gate of the main shrine were two steles carved in the late thirteenth century with the *Tao* and *Te* sections of the text.

Facing the gate was the shrine hall honoring their author. On the right, a smaller shrine honored the later Taoist philosophers Chuang-tzu and Lieh-tzu, and on the left, another small shrine honored T'ai-pai, the evening star of the western horizon. I stopped to talk with a monk sitting on its steps. His name was Jen Fa-chou, and he turned out to be the assistant abbot of Loukuantai as well as deputy director of the province's Taoist association. He said that when he first arrived at Loukuantai in 1958 the number of monks and nuns had declined to one hundred and fifty. There had been more than five hundred before "Liberation," as the Communists like to call their 1949 takeover. Only about a dozen managed to weather the Cultural Revolution (1965–1976) at the temple. In addition to chasing out most of the temple's monks and nuns, Jen said the Red Guards destroyed all the buildings, and those on the knoll had only recently been rebuilt.

Behind Lao-tzu's shrine, we followed a flight of steps down the north slope of the knoll to an adjoining shrine honoring the Lady of the Southern Dipper, who looks after human destinies to ensure that people live out their allotted span of years. Since my son, Redcloud, was born on the festival of her husband, Lord of the Northern Dipper, I lit a handful of incense. It didn't compare, though, with the fragrance of the peach blossoms outside.

Behind her shrine, we followed another flight of steps down to yet another shrine, this one honoring the Princess of Rainbow-Colored Clouds, bestower of children, whom I also thanked, for my daughter, Iris.

On our way back to the entrance, we walked along the arcades of the courtyards through which we had just passed. The walls were lined with steles carved with poems, calligraphy, and even drawings by famous visitors of the past. Among the ninth-century visitors was the poet Pai Chu-yi, who left this poem. It begins by quoting two lines that appear near the end of the five-thousand-word text of the *Tao-teching*:

> *those who speak don't know*
> *those who know keep silent*
> *these are Lao-tzu's words you say*
> *but if they mean Lao-tzu knew*
> *why did he speak five thousand words*

Back down in the main courtyard, we ordered noodles and I read the brochure visitors receive at the main gate. In 1982 the land around Loukuantai, 640 hectares' worth, had been placed under the control of the provincial government's forest administration and planted with groves of bamboo, black locust, walnut, and pine. At a distance of seventy kilometers, or about three hours by bus, Loukuantai was a little too far from Sian for most tourists. And the government was apparently turning it into a center for forest research.

As I looked at the brochure and wondered what was behind the layout of Loukuantai's scattered groups of buildings, the thought occurred that the arrangement might have been intended to represent the three internal spiritual centers, or *tan-t'ien,* where Taoists concentrate the circulation of their inner breath. If this were true, then the site of the former imperial shrines on the plain two kilometers to the north would represent the lower spiritual center, just below the navel; the nearby knoll where Lao-tzu delivered his talks on the Tao would represent the middle center, near the heart; and the mountain shrine two kilometers south of the knoll would represent the upper center, in the head, toward which we now turned our attention.

From the courtyard, the trail began with a series of brick steps, then wandered along the path of the most recent rain. An hour later, after receiving ritual stings from a swarm of guardian bees, we finally reached Lientanlu, or Cinnabar Cauldron, where Lao-tzu is said to have smelted his elixir before departing for the land of immortals.

The solitary shrine was only big enough for an altar and three stools, on one of which sat an old Taoist nun. She said she sat there all day every day taking care of the shrine for the temple in exchange for flour and other necessities. Her name was Chang, and she was from the Nanyang area of Hupei Province. As our eyes adjusted to the light, we could see that she had bound feet, which had left her crippled since childhood. She said she went down the mountain once or twice a year on special occasions. She was seventy-nine and had been a nun for more than fifty years. For the last twenty years, she had lived as a hermit, first on Taipaishan to the west and more recently on the mountain overlooking Loukuantai. She said she preferred to live alone in

Taoist nun at Cinnabar Cauldron.

order to practice meditation. But the winters, she said, were rough, and the roof of the shrine leaked when it rained. A hundred meters farther up the trail was an adobe hut with a thatched roof that served as her home. It had been built several decades earlier by another hermit.

When I asked about other hermits, she said there had been quite a few in the area when she first arrived ten years ago, but most had died, moved elsewhere, or returned to the temple. She said she knew of an old Buddhist monk who lived in a hut three ridges away. That would put him, I reckoned, somewhere near the slopes of Szufangtai.

I enjoyed talking with her but wished I could have understood more of the Hupei dialect. We returned to the courtyard below and the subject of Loukuantai's symmetry. In addition to the three spiritual centers, all of which were two kilometers apart, on a north-south axis, Loukuantai also had two east-west wings, reaching about six kilometers in either direction. The form that I saw emerging reminded me of the legendary bird at the beginning of the *Chuangtzu:*

In the North Sea lives a fish thousands of miles long called K'un. It changes into a bird thousands of miles wide called P'eng. As it soars heavenward, its wings look like a cloud-filled sky. Once it leaves the sea, it heads south for the Pond of Heaven.

P'eng's right wing included a series of structures that ended at a place called West Loukuantai. The foreign affairs police in Sian told us that West Loukuantai was "too dangerous" and thus off-limits to foreigners. We assumed this meant it was located near some sort of military installation. But according to the monks, the only sights at West Loukuantai were a small temple and Lao-tzu's grave.

I don't know when the story of Lao-tzu's grave originated, but when Szu-ma Ch'ien wrote his biography of the great sage around 100 B.C., he said Lao-tzu continued west and finally disappeared through the Sankuan Pass—a two-days' ride from Loukuantai. A Taoist monk at the temple told me that both stories were probably true. Taoists, he said, shed their bones like a snake sheds its skin, and Lao-tzu could easily have left his mortal coil at Loukuantai before slipping away.

Since we were unable to visit Loukuantai's western wing, we turned our attention to its eastern counterpart, which ends at a place called Yangtienchih, the Pond That Looks toward Heaven. No one said the pond or its nearby shrine was off-limits, and a man who sold noodles and incense at the main gate agreed to guide us. He hadn't been there in over ten years, he said, but he remembered the way. We headed down the east side of the knoll and were soon walking through fields of millet sprouts.

About one kilometer from the knoll, we passed a stele that stood alone among the sprouts. Our guide said that it was all the Red Guards had left of a large temple once occupying the spot. Beyond the stele, we crossed the Tien River, walked past a village of mud houses, and headed into the mountains.

A few minutes later, we reached a knoll once crowned by a shrine to Yuan-shih-t'ien, God of the Beginning, of whom Lao-tzu was an incarnation. Our guide lit incense and candles in front of a stele, which was all that remained of the shrine, and we went on.

Along the trail, we met several woodcutters. One of them said that the last Taoist nun living at Yangtienchih had left the previous year for the distant peak of Taipaishan, where she had more room to plant vegetables and more solitude.

An hour later, we reached the saddle and took a side trail to a small shrine on the summit. It was eight-sided, like the Taoist *pa-kua* figure that represents the eight trigrams in the *I Ching,* or Book of Changes. It is called Hsichenting, Resting Place of Immortals, and is where Lao-tzu is said to have practiced meditation during his stay at Loukuantai. Any statues or ritual paraphernalia it might once have contained had been removed. We went back down to the saddle and continued into a nearby mountain village of six households strung out along the northern side of a rush-filled pond. This was Yangtienchih, the Pond That Looks toward Heaven.

We were welcomed by a farmer in a blue sailor's cap who had such ruddy cheeks I thought he was Dutch at first. He led us between two farmhouses and opened the shrine that the Taoist nun had abandoned the year before. Inside, the walls were covered by paintings showing the rise and fall of the Chou dynasty and Lao-tzu's passage through the world. The main statue was of the Jade Emperor, who took over leadership of the Taoist pantheon after the God of the Beginning got things started, and on the right was a statue of Lao-tzu. Made of clay and covered by a red shawl, it had an aura unlike any other statue I'd ever seen of the sage. While my guide lit incense and candles in front of the Jade Emperor, I took Lao-tzu's picture.

Before the Cultural Revolution, the area around the pond had been occupied by a temple and a large community of monks and nuns. The small deserted shrine is all that remains.

After the farmer locked the door, he invited us into his house for bowls of hot sugar-water. When we had quenched our thirst, his wife started making fresh noodles, the farmer began peeling potatoes, and I went back outside and lit what remained of a cigar. On either side of the farmer's house, magpies squawked from their nests in tall birch trees. The pond that took up most of the village area was full of dry rushes that rattled in the wind. As I walked around to the other side, a couple of frogs dived in. The village children told me they raised *wu-szu* ("five-color") fish in the pond. I wondered if they might be some kind of trout, but all I could see were rushes.

Beyond the pond to the south, the saddle dropped abruptly, and the mountain ridges behind Loukuantai were visible for about thirty kilometers. About twenty kilometers away to the southwest, I could see the 2,600-meter peak of Szufangtai and scanned the area around it with my binoculars. It was too far away, though, to see any sign of smoke or thatch. Immediately to the west of Szufangtai was Tung-laochunling, and somewhere in the haze another thirty kilometers west of Tunglaochunling was the great white rock of Taipaishan — at 3,800 meters, the highest peak of the Chungnan Mountains.

The cigar didn't last long, and our guide was anxious to go home. We filled up on noodles and potatoes, thanked the farmer and his wife for their hospitality and headed back to Loukuantai. Halfway down the mountain we surprised two partridges, and along the trail, we stopped to pick little white stars growing out of the ground. Everywhere there were peach trees in bloom. Back at the hostel, we washed away the sweat of the trail with a bucket of cold water.

Before retiring for the night, I asked the local cultural affairs official about the Taoists who had lived there in the past. He said a detailed history had been completed but was still awaiting a certain amount of editing. It was expected to be available in another two years.

When I asked about Loukuantai's present residents, an old monk with a single, incredibly long tooth left in his mouth suggested we talk with the abbot. He pointed us to a nearby group of buildings. It was a former military barracks, and there were still red stars over the doors. The monk said the place was slated for demolition, and a new, larger monastery would replace the barracks sometime during the next five years.

We found the abbot's assistant in the kitchen, and he escorted us into a reception room where we were introduced to the abbot, Jen Fa-jung. Master Jen was from neighboring Kansu Province and had a long black beard characteristic of Chinese from the northwest part of the country. He was also director of the Shensi Taoist Association. I later learned from other Taoists that he was one of the most respected masters in China.

After we exchanged introductions, he gave me a copy of his com-

Taoist monks at Loukuantai.

mentary to Lao-tzu's *Taoteching,* the book that had led us to Louku-antai. During our forays into the Chungnan Mountains, I visited Master Jen twice, and I've excerpted parts of both interviews below. Since Master Jen was more careful of his words than he had been earlier in the Chinese Taoist Association's periodical *Chungkuo Taochiao* (Chinese Taoism) (fall 1989, vol. 10, pp. 12–15), I've paraphrased some of his written remarks to amplify his answers.

Master Jen didn't look very old, and I was surprised when he said he was sixty. I asked him how long he had been a monk.

Jen: I was nineteen when I left home. I've been a monk more than forty years. When I first told my parents, they didn't approve. But they finally accepted my decision, and I went to live at Lungmentung northwest of here. I stayed there for three years. It wasn't easy. But if you live at a Taoist temple, and you're not willing to suffer for a few years, no one will teach you.

Q: Were you here during the Cultural Revolution?

Jen: Yes. I've been here for the past thirty years.

Q: What happened?

Jen: The Red Guards came and destroyed the shrines and statues and burned our books. They also beat up the monks. They harassed us for ten years. [According to Jen's report in *Chungkuo Taochiao,* extensive damage was done to almost all Taoist temples in Shensi Province during the ten years of the Cultural Revolution. Since 1982, ten of the seventy-two Taoist shrines and temples in the province have been partially restored. Of these, only Loukuantai, Huashan, and Pahsienkung in Sian received financial assistance from the government. In the case of Loukuantai, the figure was 130,000 RMB, or twenty-five thousand dollars; for Pahsienkung the figure was 150,000 RMB; the figure for Huashan was not reported.]

Q: When did conditions begin to improve?

Jen: In 1979, after the Third Plenary of the Eleventh Party Congress.

Since then, conditions have slowly gotten better. [In his report, Jen says that in the ten years since the new religious policy was announced, "leftist thinking" has continued to hinder religious development, especially in the transfer of control over religious sites. The problem in Shensi Province, he says, is especially serious at Loukuantai, Chungyang Temple, Huashan, and Paiyunshan in northern Shensi. Jen stressed that it was to everyone's advantage for religious sites to be under the control of religious practitioners and that without such control religious communities were unlikely to achieve the government's goal of self-sufficiency.]

Q: Does the temple provide monks and nuns who live here with money to help cover their personal expenses?

Jen: Yes. Right now everyone gets about 20 RMB [four dollars] a month from the money we earn by selling entrance tickets, incense, and handicrafts. The monks at Loukuantai have always combined practice and work. We also plant vegetables like turnips and cabbages and potatoes, and we wear the same set of clothes all year. We don't need much money. We'd rather use what little money we make to repair the temple or buy books.

Q: How is this temple organized?

Jen: It's very similar to a Buddhist temple. Both religions have temples, and our names for different functions in a temple are the same. The administration is the same. Every religion has an organization. We have one too. We have rules. But practice is up to the individual. [The present national Taoist association drew up regulations governing Taoist temples in 1987. Every temple is left to organize itself according to local conditions and to support itself by any means that don't conflict with the public welfare. Responsibilities are said to be assigned and income distributed according to democratic principles. The current mottoes advanced by the association are "Let each temple support itself" and "Make the temple a home." In his report, Jen notes that after 1949 ordination of new monks was forbidden by the Communist government. This policy was overturned in 1978 at the Third

Plenary, and the Taoist association was reestablished in the same year. Since then, the twenty-three major centers of the Chuan Chen sect and another two hundred smaller temples have been brought into the association. Jen later told me that the current number of Taoist monks and nuns in China was around ten thousand. Association officials at the national headquarters at Paiyun Temple in Peking, however, told me the figure was closer to three thousand and that the number of Taoist temples in China was around five hundred, most of which were too small to establish membership in the association.]

Q: What changes have occurred in Taoism in recent decades?

Jen: Chinese Taoism was divided many centuries ago into the Chuan Chen [Complete Truth] and Cheng Yi [True Unity] sects. The Chuan Chen sect has been the major sect in the north, and the Cheng Yi sect has been more popular in the south. The Cheng Yi sect is a lay sect with centers in places like Szechuan Province, Shanghai, and Lunghushan in Kiangsi Province. It's also called the Way of the Heavenly Teachers. Members can marry, eat meat, and drink wine. They live at home. The Chuan Chen sect cuts itself off from the red dust. Its members live in monasteries. We belong to the Chuan Chen sect. In the past, as I said, the Chuan Chen sect predominated in the north, but now the Cheng Yi sect is more popular. This is the biggest change.

Q: Which sect controls the Taoist association?

Jen: Neither. The association includes both sects, both lay believers and monastic practitioners. It doesn't ignore or emphasize either or interfere with either. The association doesn't interfere with any form of belief or practice. [A casual glance through the publications of the national association makes it clear that its senior officials and directors are mostly monks and nuns of the Chuan Chen sect.]

Q: If a person wants to study with a particular Taoist master, is this a matter for the student and master to decide, or is the permission of the association necessary?

Jen: People can do what they want. The association can't interfere. [According to other Taoist monks we talked with, the local association decides where disciples can study and in what temples monks and nuns can live.]

Q: Are young people still interested in becoming monks or nuns?

Jen: Yes. More than twenty of the fifty monks currently living here are under thirty. [In his report, Jen states that despite a lack of young monks and nuns at temples in the province, the government won't let young people interested in becoming monks and nuns stay at a temple for more than a brief period unless they first change their household registration, a process always difficult and often impossible. This bureaucratic restriction, he says, is making it hard for temples to attract young Taoists.]

Q: Do you ever have classes?

Jen: Yes, sometimes. But not many people these days are interested in Taoism. [Jen's report states that periodic classes on Taoism during the previous two years at Loukuantai attracted between thirty and forty people, while a three-week class on *ch'i-kung*, or Taoist yoga, attracted more than three hundred people, two hundred of whom were from outside the province.]

Q: Do you have problems teaching people Taoism nowadays?

Jen: To find people who truly believe is the biggest problem we have. Taoism teaches us to reduce our desires and to lead quiet lives. People willing to reduce their desires or cultivate tranquillity in this modern age are very few. This is the age of desire. Also, people learn much more slowly now. Their minds aren't as simple. They're too complicated.

Q: I understand that much of the advanced instruction in Taoism is secret and only transmitted to a few disciples. Is this true?

Jen: Yes, to some extent. A Taoist master who accepts a disciple might test him for several decades before he teaches him everything he knows. Not many disciples have that kind of determination.

Q: Is there religious freedom in China now?

Jen: Yes. We can practice however we want. We can practice in the mountains, or we can practice in cities, in temples, or at home.

Q: Do any Taoists practice by themselves in these mountains?

Jen: Yes. There are still some, but not as many as before. Many of their huts were destroyed during the Cultural Revolution. Several years ago, one hermit living near here achieved immortality at the age of ninety-six. And two years ago, another became an immortal at the age of one hundred and forty. I know of several others living in the foothills of Taipaishan, but I hardly ever see them.

Q: Did you ever live as a hermit?

Jen: Yes. But for less than three years. It was a good experience. Sooner or later all Taoists have to live alone for a period to concentrate on their practice. To practice you have to find a secluded place, at least in the beginning. But the important thing is to learn to still your mind. Once you can do that, you can live anywhere, even in a noisy city.

Q: I've noticed that many religious centers such as this have also begun to attract tourists. Does this affect your practice?

Jen: Yes. It's not so quiet anymore. It's much harder to practice. But that's just the way it is. We have to make use of whatever means of support we can find to rebuild our centers and to train new monks and nuns.

Q: What's the goal of Taoist practice?

Jen: Man's nature is the same as the nature of heaven. Heaven gives birth to all creatures, and they all go different directions. But sooner or later they return to the same place. The goal of this universe, its

Jen Fa-jung, **abbot of Loukuantai.**

highest goal, is nothingness. Nothingness means return. Nothingness is the body of the Tao. Not only man, but plants and animals and all living things are part of this body, are made of this body, this body of nothingness. Everything is one with nothingness. There aren't two things in this universe. To realize this is the goal not only of Taoism but also of Buddhism. Everything in this world changes. Taoists and Buddhists seek that which doesn't change. This is why they don't seek fame or fortune. They seek only the Tao, which is the nothingness of which we are all created and to which we all return. Our goal is to be one with this natural process.

Q: How does a person reach this goal?

Jen: It's a matter of stages. There are many degrees of achievement, and it's hard to reach the goal. But once you have this as your goal, you just keep going, step by step, stage by stage. Everyone has different capabilities, but the goal is the same. The goal is to become immortal, to return to the body of the Tao. If you practice, eventually you'll succeed. In Buddhism, enlightenment is the main goal. In Taoism, enlightenment is secondary. You still have to practice after you're enlightened until gradually and very naturally you become one with the Tao. If you don't succeed in this life, you'll have another chance next life. But people who don't practice don't get another chance, their life force ends. Taoist practice involves the creation of an immortal body that separates from this mortal body at death. You can visit Lao-tzu's grave. He left his bones there when he became an immortal. Our goal is the same as his, to become one with the Tao.

Q: Is it necessary to be a monk or nun?

Jen: The important thing is to lead an upright life. You don't have to be a monk or nun to do this. It doesn't do any good to be a monk or nun if you don't keep the precepts. What's important is to keep the precepts. But anyone who leads an upright life does this. This is the basis of practice. The precepts are the demands you place on yourself. Precepts make practice possible. If you don't make demands on yourself, you won't get anywhere in your practice.

Q: Have the forms of practice changed today?

Jen: No, they're the same now as they were for Lao-tzu. People haven't changed; neither has the Tao. The way we live our lives, the way we meditate, the way we cultivate our life force is still the same.

Q: What exactly is the status of Lao-tzu in Taoism? Many people think of him as a philosopher, not as the founder of a religion.

Jen: That's the modern view. But Lao-tzu can't be separated from religion. The Chinese people have always believed in the Tao, and this belief has led them to cultivate various forms of religious practice. Do you think Lao-tzu talked about the Tao but didn't believe or cultivate it? He knew that everything in the universe comes from the Tao and that it's impossible to leave the Tao. There wasn't an organized religion then, but it was the same Tao.

Chapter Five

Sound
of the
Crane

*I*n its historic form Taoism may have originated, as Taoists claim, at the western end of the Chungnan Mountains on Loukuantai. But in its prehistoric form Taoism flourished much earlier at the other end of the Chungnan Mountains on Huashan. Huashan's significance for Taoists, though, goes back even before prehistoric times to the beginning of creation.

In the beginning, Chaos split into yin and yang. When these split again, into greater and lesser yin and greater and lesser yang, the combined interaction of these four forces produced the myriad creatures, the first of which was P'an-ku. As soon as he was born, P'an-ku picked up a mallet and chisel and spent the rest of his life creating the space between heaven and earth in which we all live. Instead of seven days, it took him eighteen thousand years. And when he finally lay down and died, his body became the five sacred mountains: his head became the eastern mountain; his arms became the northern and southern mountains; his belly, the central mountain; and his feet, the western mountain.

After a few millennia of weathering, P'an-ku's feet came to resemble a blossom rising from foliage of stone, and the early Chinese called

the western mountain Huashan, Flower Mountain. It bloomed in the
heart of China's earliest tribal and civilized cultures, and the Chinese
still refer to themselves as Hua-jen, people of Hua, indicating the importance this mountain once had for their ancestors.

Huashan had a special power to attract veneration. Its form was
unique among mountains. And to climb it required great courage and
great desire, desire not of the flesh but of the spirit. For Huashan was
one of China's earliest spiritual centers, a place where shamans came
to seek visions. One such shaman was Huang-ti, the Yellow Emperor,
who climbed Huashan on several occasions to talk with the gods.
When Huang-ti rode off on a dragon to join his fellow immortals
around 2600 B.C., his earthly power as overlord of the tribes in north
China passed into the hands of the White Emperor, Pai-ti.

Although Pai-ti established his court far to the east in the Yellow
River floodplain, one branch of his descendants moved near Huashan
and began holding regular sacrifices to their esteemed ancestor here.
In succeeding centuries, the sage emperors Yao, Shun, and Yu the
Great also visited Huashan. The *Chuangtzu* describes a visit by Yao,
around 2400 B.C., during which the caretaker of the sacrificial center
faulted the sage emperor for worrying about the blessings of many
sons, wealth, and long life:

> At first I thought you were a sage, but now I see you are merely another
> lord. Men are all created by Heaven and receive from Heaven their ap-
> pointed lot. What concern should you have that your sons won't receive
> theirs? And wealth can be shared with others. What cause is there in
> that for worry? A sage lives like a quail on scattered grain. When he
> flies, he leaves no trace. When the Tao prevails in the world, he lives
> in harmony with others. When the Tao doesn't prevail, he cultivates
> his virtue in seclusion. And after a thousand years, when he finally tires
> of this world, he leaves to join the immortals and rides a cloud all the
> way to Heaven, where such worries don't arise and misfortune has no
> hold. (Chap. 12)

The place where Huashan's Taoist caretaker gave Yao this advice is
known as Huafeng. It's about three kilometers east of the present

county seat of Huayin. Unfortunately, the last artifacts of the former sacrificial center were destroyed in 1958 during Mao's Great Leap Forward, and the site is now better known for the neolithic remains discovered there since then. Two other shrines have also disappeared. One built at the beginning of the Chou dynasty south of Huayin has become Huashan High School. Another, built during the early Han dynasty at the mouth of nearby Huangfu Gorge, was washed away by floods several centuries ago.

A fourth and final shrine was built around A.D. 160 just east of Huayin. Known as Hsiyuehmiao, Temple of the Western Mountain, it remains, I'm told, an imposing monument to Chinese craftsmanship. Its main hall, as one would expect, is dedicated to Pai-ti, whose descendants became the protectors of the mountain some forty-five hundred years ago. In addition to numerous buildings, the grounds include a grove of cedars said to have been planted long before the original shrine was built. The entire site is enclosed by a wall and is off-limits to foreigners. It has been used as a military headquarters and barracks for decades, which is probably why it survived the Red Guards.

But no temple, however imposing, can ever compare with a mountain like Huashan. On our first trip to China, we saw a picture of Huashan in a flight magazine. It was so dreamlike, we couldn't imagine actually being in such a place. But that was before we discovered hermits in the Chungnan Mountains and realized Huashan was at their eastern end. On our second trip, Steve and I decided it was time to climb P'an-ku's feet.

*I*t was the middle of August and the middle of summer rains. After waiting for the sun in Sian for a week, we decided to take a chance. Four hours and 120 kilometers later, we were looking up Huashan's one muddy street into the mountains. We could see blue sky.

We dropped our gear in a cheap hotel and set out to explore. Past a gauntlet of tourist shops, we entered the main gate of Yuchuanyuan, or Jade Spring Temple. It was built in the middle of the eleventh century as a shrine to Ch'en T'uan, who had lived here as a hermit the century before. Besides inspiring early Neo-Confucian thinkers with his *Wuchitu* (Diagram of the Limitless), Ch'en cultivated Taoist meditation and was known for his ability to remain in a sleeplike trance for months at a time. His reclining figure can still be seen in a small cave on the west side of the grounds. For a small donation, the old lady in charge of the shrine let us inside. We ran our hands over Ch'en's stone figure. It had been touched by so many hands since it was carved in 1103, it looked and felt like polished black jade.

Nearby was a pavilion that Ch'en had built on top of a boulder. And in front of the boulder grew the lone survivor of four cuttings Ch'en planted from the tree beneath which the Buddha was born. According to one Taoist legend, after Lao-tzu joined the immortals, he was reborn as Shakyamuni. The Red Guards apparently thought they had destroyed the last of the four trees, but its gnarled stump was still sending forth shoots.

Just outside the entrance to the main shrine, a stele carved with a representation of Huashan caught our attention. It was cracked in the middle, but we studied it as best as we could through the protective bars and the dust on its surface. If the mountain was anything like the picture, Steve and I were going to lose some weight.

On the east side of the temple grounds, we stopped again at a stone marker next to another boulder. This was one of the many graves of Hua T'uo, China's greatest medical genius, who died in A.D. 207 at the age of ninety-seven. For many years Hua lived in a cave on Huashan and collected herbs for which the mountain is still famous: special varieties of Solomon's seal, ginseng, asarum, and acorus, to name a few. Among his accomplishments was the use of acupuncture and hemp-based anesthetics to perform surgery. He is also credited with devising five forms of exercise that were later developed into the basic styles of Chinese martial arts. Although Hua repeatedly refused official posts, he was forced to treat the chronic headaches of Ts'ao Ts'ao, who had usurped the throne at the end of the Han dynasty. When he refused to continue the treatments, he was ordered killed lest he reveal information about Ts'ao Ts'ao's health to his enemies, who were many.

Beyond Hua T'uo's grave and the eastern wall of Jade Spring Temple were two smaller Taoist monasteries. The first was Shihertung

Temple, where most visiting monks stay. We walked past its rusted metal gate and after another hundred meters entered the brick and wooden doorway of Hsienku Temple. A Chinese friend in Sian had told us this was where Master Hsieh lived. We found him propped up in bed treating his arthritic knees with a heat lamp. Once renowned for his skill in martial arts, he now had trouble walking. His room included two plank beds pushed together and covered by a mosquito net, an arrangement I found in the rooms of other monks who used their beds for meditation and study as well as sleep. There were two chests containing books and clothes, a desk, two folding chairs, a new color TV (presented by the provincial government for help in cultural preservation), and a scroll with the Chinese character for patience on the wall. After exchanging introductions, I handed Master Hsieh a cigar and lit one myself. While we smoked, he told me about his life.

Hsieh's parents were originally from Shantung Province but had moved south in the waning years of the Ch'ing dynasty to find work. He was born in Anhui Province and became a monk while he was still in his teens. After the standard three-year apprenticeship, he came to Huashan to practice. At the time of our meeting, he had just turned eighty and had been living at Huashan for sixty years. His arthritic knees aside, he was unusually robust, and his mind was as clear as the sky after a long rain. I asked him about Taoism.

Hsieh: Lao-tzu said to cultivate tranquillity and detachment. To be natural. To be natural means not to force things. When you act natural, you get what you need. But to know what's natural, you have to cultivate tranquillity. Huashan has long been famous as a center of Taoism because it's quiet. There used to be a lot of hermits here. But now the mountain has been developed for tourism. The tranquillity is gone, and so are the hermits.

Q: Where did they go?

Hsieh: That's hard to say. Hermits want to be left alone, so they're not easy to find. They prefer isolation. Some of them returned to the cities. Others moved deeper into the Chungnan Mountains, where it's

Master Hsieh with author on steps of Hsienku Temple.

still quiet. But even if you found them, they probably wouldn't talk to you. They don't like to be disturbed. They prefer to meditate. They're not interested in conversation. They might say a few words to you then close their door and not come out again.

Q: But they have to eat. Sooner or later they have to come out again, don't they?

Hsieh: That depends. Sometimes they eat once a day, sometimes once every three days, sometimes once a week. As long as they're able to nourish their inner energy, they're fine, they don't need food. They might meditate for one day, two days, a week, even several weeks. You might have to wait a long time before they come out again.

Q: Aren't they interested in teaching others?

Hsieh: Yes. But before you can teach others, you have to cultivate yourself. You have to know something before you can teach something. You can't explain inner cultivation just because you know words in books. You have to discover what they mean first.

Q: If people can't learn Taoism from hermits, can they learn from monks in temples?

Hsieh: You can't learn just by visiting a temple. You have to live there for at least three years and help with the daily work. If you can stand the hardship and privation, after three years you can ask one of the monks to be your teacher. It's not easy. You have to have a clear head and a quiet mind. As I said before, it takes at least three years of physical training before your mind is quiet enough to understand the Tao.

Q: In the last twenty or thirty years, the political situation in China has been difficult. What effect has this had on Taoism?

Hsieh: I'd rather not talk about this.

Q: Were Taoist monks and nuns able to continue their practice here at Huashan?

Hsieh: Please, I'd rather not talk about this.

Q: When you were living on the mountain, you must have needed certain things from down below. How did you get them?

Hsieh: We had to carry everything on our backs. I made quite a few trips when I was younger. Nowadays, visitors sometimes give the monks money, and the monks pay others to carry things up so they can concentrate on their practice.

Q: Has there been much change in the number of Taoists living here?

Hsieh: When I first came here, there were forty or fifty old masters on the mountain, more than two hundred monks and nuns, and too many novices to count. Now, only a few of us are left.

Q: What happened to them all?

Hsieh: Some died. Most left. Most returned to their families.

Q: What about the temples?

Hsieh: They're for tourists. Everything has changed. The tourist officials are in charge now.

I asked Hsieh if I could talk with Master Hsing, Hsienku Temple's ninety-year-old abbot. Suddenly Hsieh turned serious and said it would not be convenient. I felt the forty-year shadow of Liberation. Apparently, Hsing had a problem—and it wasn't his health. On our way out, we saw Master Hsing giving instructions to a youth who had come all the way from Chekiang Province to carve dragons and cranes for the temple. Steve and I bowed in greeting and left.

Later, Master Hsieh joined us for a spartan dinner in our hotel room. He excused himself for not being able to talk freely in the temple. The walls, he said, had ears. He said things were getting worse for Taoists, not better. Religion was being resurrected by the government for the purpose of promoting tourism. He said that Taoism was just about dead, that in all of China there were fewer than a hundred and fifty Taoist monks and nuns who could qualify as masters.

Historians of the Han dynasty say there were thirteen hundred Taoist masters of note during the reign of Emperor Ming two thousand years ago when the country's population was around 50 million. In other words, when the population was one-twentieth its current level, there were ten times as many Taoist masters in China. A sad state, indeed, for what many Chinese still call their national religion.

On the way back to his temple, Master Hsieh showed us the entrance to the local hot showers. They were in a veterans' home that housed several hundred soldiers injured during China's border conflict with Vietnam. We said good-bye at the gate, and Hsieh hobbled slowly back to Hsienku Temple, supporting himself with his cane.

Later, as Steve and I walked back to our room under a bright moon, I wondered if Hsieh was among the last in the long line of Taoists who had been coming to Huashan for the past five thousand years, a line that included Mao Meng, who came to Huashan more than two thousand years ago. After he achieved immortality and disappeared on the back of a dragon in broad daylight, his descendants traveled to the eastern coastal province of Kiangsu, where they established on Mao-shan one of China's most famous Taoist centers. The flower and the wind are old friends. If Huashan seeds could reach eastern China, perhaps they could cross the ocean.

The next morning, Steve and I woke to sunlight for the first time in more than a week. We went back through the courtyard of Jade Spring Temple and began our hike up the gorge that led to the summit. Even after a week of continuous rain, the stream was as clear as rippling glass. No trace of mud. Only granite boulders and granite sand. The *Shanhaiching,* the shaman's ancient guide to the mountains, says there's a kind of rock good for washing the body and curing skin diseases on a mountain near Huashan. The river's white sand looked like it could scour away the red dust of illusion.

It was the height of summer, and the morning sun was intense. We were glad to have the shade of the gorge as we began what turned out to be an eight-hour climb. After several kilometers, the main gorge opened up at Shaloping, which was named for two huge *sal* trees that once grew here. It was between two such trees that Shakyamuni (who some Taoists claim was Lao-tzu in another body) entered nirvana. The trees used to stand before a shrine on the west wall of the gorge. Caretakers of a nearby hostel told us they were cut down during the Cultural Revolution, but local records say they were washed away during a flood in 1884.

Across the stream, a number of caves had been carved into the gorge's east wall in an area known as Hsiaoshangfang (Lower Shangfang). They were overgrown now and must have been abandoned years ago. During the T'ang dynasty, the younger sister of Emperor Hsuan-tsung lived in one of the caves farther up the cliff at Chungshangfang (Middle Shangfang). Higher still were the caves of Tashangfang (Upper Shangfang), somewhere in the clouds. According to the Buddhist travel-diarist Kao Ho-nien, Taoist hermits were living at all three levels when he visited in 1904.

We continued along the gorge and paused again at the base of Maonutung Peak, named for a woman who cultivated the Tao. Her original name was Yu-chiang, and she once lived in a cave near the summit. When the First Emperor of the Ch'in dynasty died in 210 B.C., a number of his concubines were chosen to join him in eternal repose. Yu-chiang was among those selected to play the heavenly zither. But the night before she was to be taken to the emperor's mausoleum near Lishan, an old eunuch helped her escape to Huashan.

Later, she met a Taoist master who taught her how to survive on a diet of pine needles and spring water, how to visualize the seven stars of the Big Dipper that connect a person's life force, and how to walk the shaman's Walk of Yu. Through such cultivation, her body became covered with long green hair, and people started calling her Mao-nu, Down-haired Maiden. Since that time, hunters have periodically reported hearing the sound of her zither and seeing a flash of green near this peak where she once lived. I looked around. Beside me on a boulder, a blue-tailed lizard was enjoying the morning sun.

A few hundred meters past Maonutung, Huashan Gorge ended. We were at Chingkoping, the location of Tungtao Temple. The small

Ancient hermit caves of Lower Shangfang at Shaloping, on the way up Huashan.

羅立諸峯

南縣縣華
州縣縣峯
剌參繩觀
峙員福
陳
聯
福

明星玉女

temple is a recent version of an ancient shrine honoring Chiu-t'ien Hsuan-nu, the Dark Maiden of the Nine Heavens. According to Taoist legend, she taught Huang-ti how to overcome his opponents in battle. As a result, he defeated Ch'ih Yu at the Battle of Cholu, a hundred kilometers northwest of Huashan, and became the first patriarch of Chinese civilization.

Chingkoping is also the halfway point between the mouth of Huashan Gorge and the summit. It's 5.5 kilometers either way. But the next half is the hardest. The trail seems to go straight up, and in some places the gradient is, in fact, ninety degrees. Although shamans and Taoists had reportedly been climbing Huashan for centuries, if not millennia, it wasn't until the third century B.C. that King Chao-hsiang of the state of Ch'in made the mountain accessible to ordinary mortals. In order to bring down an ancient pine from the summit to make into a huge chessboard, he had his workmen install a series of iron chains and ladders.

The view from Chingkoping suggests that the author of the *Shanhaiching* was not exaggerating when he described Huashan as "sheer on all sides, as if carved by a knife, five thousand fathoms high." After passing Turnback Rock, we began the ascent and wondered how anyone could have made it to the top without the chains. I went ahead and didn't see Steve again until two hours later, when I looked back down at the dragon spine of Tsanglung Ridge.

When he visited Huashan in the T'ang dynasty, the Confucian scholar and poet Han Yu got halfway across this ridge and became paralyzed with fear. Like all scholars, he never went anywhere without his writing kit. In desperation, he wrote a letter of farewell and dropped it over the edge. Help eventually arrived, and he was carried down the mountain. Since then, the path along the ridge has been made wider and lined with chains for safety. Still, as I was about to yell down to Steve, I suddenly stopped, terrified by the thought that my voice would fall into the abyss and take me with it.

Through binoculars I watched Steve frighten several hikers by climbing over the chains to get a better angle for a shot of Huashan's

North Peak, whose rocky pinnacle was jutting through swirling mist. Standing next to me, three commercial artists from Canton were looking down at the same scene, two of them painting in oils, the third in pastels. Chinese ink was nowhere in sight.

A few minutes later, I reached the archway of Chinsuokuan, the traditional entrance to the summit and the place where the trail finally divides. Master Hsieh had advised us to stay overnight at the lodge on East Peak, so I took the trail to the left. After a few minutes, I stopped to share a small watermelon with a porter who made his living carrying things up the mountain. Loads varied, he said, between forty and fifty kilos, and the fee for one trip was 10 RMB, two dollars. I tried to heft his load. It felt like a ton.

This was also where the oaks and pines began. I stretched out in their shade and watched the clouds appear from nowhere and disappear into nothingness. Listening to the wind in the trees, I thought of Po Ya and Chung Tzu-ch'i. Whenever Po Ya played the zither, Chung Tzu-ch'i always knew what was in Po Ya's heart: sometimes it was high mountains, sometimes flowing water. When Chung Tzu-ch'i died, Po Ya smashed his zither and never played again. The wind, I thought, was thinking about high mountains.

Finally, I got up and climbed the rest of the way to Middle Peak. Like North Peak, this was more of a promontory than a peak. Huashan has only three true peaks, but these two are often included for numerological reasons. Taoists are fond of applications for the concept of the five elements: water, fire, wood, metal, and earth; black, red, green, white, and yellow; north, south, east, west, and middle.

Middle Peak is also called Jade Maiden Peak after the daughter of Duke Mu of the state of Ch'in. The duke's daughter came to Huashan twenty-six hundred years ago with her husband, the flute master Hsiao Shih. After living on the mountain for several decades, she and her husband drank an elixir of liquid jade and flew off to join the immortals. In honor of his daughter, the duke built a shrine here. It's been rebuilt many times, most recently in 1983.

From Middle Peak, the main trail to East Peak leads down a long

East Peak chess pavilion.

series of steps, then along the eastern edge of the summit's interior and up again to the peak. But there's a shortcut, and I needed a shortcut. I retraced my steps and took a side trail to Yinfeng Pavilion, where the Duke's daughter often played the pan-pipes and her husband the flute, and the wind carried their music all the way to her father's palace on the plains.

Looking south from the pavilion, I could see the handprint on East Peak left by the giant who shoved Huashan and Shouyangshan apart so that the Yellow River could turn east and flow to the sea. I scanned the gorge below with my binoculars and saw a hut in a grove of bamboo. I decided to make inquiries about it later.

I pulled myself up the final series of chains and arrived at the back gate of the temple that now serves as a lodge, just below the summit of East Peak. When I registered, I asked the man in charge about the hut I had just seen in Huangfu Gorge far below. He said it belonged to a farmer. I was disappointed, but also glad I wouldn't have to hike up another gorge for a while. I sat down outside the front gate and drank one of the beers that came up the mountain along with other necessities of life on the shoulders of local porters. Steve arrived during the second bottle and joined me in a third.

We were sitting in the spot where the picture in the flight magazine had been taken. I was amazed: the scene was real, and we were actually sitting there. Directly below us the same magic pavilion perched on the same magic promontory. The pavilion, its stools, and its chessboard-table had all been recently rebuilt, hewn from white granite. To reach it, you have to climb down chains that at one point force you to hang horizontally with your back facing the rocks several hundred meters below. More than two thousand years ago, during the reign of Emperor Wu, a Taoist by the name of Wei Shu-ch'ing was seen playing chess on this promontory with several immortals. A thousand years later, in the tenth century, Ch'en T'uan played a game of chess here with Emperor T'ai-tsu. Ch'en T'uan won, and the emperor reportedly deeded all of Huashan to him.

Steve and I watched the sinking sun illuminate the pavilion and the

Crossing Chuanchen Cliff on South Peak.

Chain ladder to cave.

moon float across the sky. We left a load of empties for some porter to carry down the next day and retired to our room.

East Peak is also known as Sunrise Peak, and we joined a hundred other visitors shivering outside before dawn. Most of them had climbed the mountain with flashlights during the night. They were on the two-day tour: leave Sian in the morning, visit the First Emperor's underground army at Lishan, climb Huashan at night, return to Sian by the following evening.

The sun rose and a hundred cameras clicked. It rose from behind a mountain where, the *Shanhaiching* says, a black pheasant lives that can be used to cure boils. The shaman's guide to the mountains also claims: "There are no birds or animals on Huashan, except for a serpent called the *fei-yi,* which has six feet and four wings and causes great droughts whenever it appears," and which we didn't see. But we did see a mouse nibbling a leaf, bumble bees visiting thistles, orange sunflowers, lilies yellower than the sun, and a family of hawks beginning their day above the peak.

After a breakfast of noodles, Steve and I began our tour of the rest of Huashan's flower-shaped summit. On the way to South Peak, we passed through the gate of a small temple at Nantienmen and came out on the peak's southern face. Huangfu and Hsienyu gorges wrap themselves around Huashan's base here, and the drop must be a thousand meters straight down. Across Hsienyu gorge to the south are the peaks of Sankungshan and Sanfengshan. Along the cliff, a trail of chains and planks lead down and across to Holao Cave, one of several hermitages carved into the mountain's sheer face by the thirteenth-century Taoist Ho Yuan-hsi.

How he found this place is a mystery. An even greater mystery is how the calligraphy above his cave got there. It proclaims this as Chu-anchen Cliff, in honor of the Chuan Chen school of Taoism. The six-inch-wide walkway to the cave is considered the most dangerous place on the mountain. A caretaker said that someone falls almost every month but added that the awareness of danger has a way of concentrating a person's abilities. I declined the thrill of danger, but Steve summoned enough courage to inch halfway down for a few pictures. As soon as he returned from the abyss, we headed for South Peak's main summit.

South Peak is also known as Wildgoose Landing. At the summit is a stone pool that contains rainwater, which presumably is what attracts the geese. It's also the highest point on Huashan, slightly under 2,200 meters. Standing here in the eighth century, the poet Li Pai remarked, "From this highest of places, my breath can reach the throne of Heaven. I regret that I didn't bring with me the profound poems of Hsieh T'iao. I had some questions for the blue sky."

From South Peak the trail winds down and across another dragon spine to West Peak. West Peak is also called Lotus Peak because of a rock said to look like a lotus leaf and because of a thousand-petal lotus flower that once grew in a pond near the summit. At the edge of the peak there's another thousand-meter drop-off into Hsienyu Gorge.

We peered over the precipice, then retraced our steps to Tsuiyun Temple, which huddles against the inside of the dragon spine.

In the main shrine hall, I met Master Hsueh T'ai-lai. He was seventy years old and had been living at the summit for forty-five years, ever since he became a monk at the age of twenty-two. Like Master Hsieh, Hsueh also had arthritic knees, but he moved with grace as he got up to offer me a cup of tea. I asked him if any other monks or nuns still lived at the summit.

Hsueh: There was another monk, Master Su. He lived on South Peak. But two months ago, he withdrew from the Taoist association and moved halfway down Huashan Gorge to Tashangfang with a disciple. I'm the only one left.

Q: If people want to live here and study with you, can they?

Hsueh: First they have to go to the Taoist association at Jade Spring Temple and ask permission. The association decides where to send people. I can't accept disciples on my own.

Q: Does the government support you?

Hsueh: No. We have to support ourselves from donations. The government sometimes helps with renovations. But we have to apply, and that takes a long time. The government, though, has relaxed its restrictions on religion. Conditions used to be very bad.

Q: Have you always lived here on West Peak?

Hsueh: No. When I first came here in 1943, I lived at Nantienmen on South Peak. I also spent quite a few years living in caves. That's why I have trouble walking now. Since Liberation, I've been sent to live at just about every temple on Huashan. We have to go wherever the association sends us.

Q: Is this a good place to practice?

Hsueh: No, not anymore. Not on Huashan. Monks who live here have to take care of visitors. We can't concentrate on our practice. No one can accomplish anything this way. People who want to practice have to go deeper into the mountains. Of course, neither the government nor the association approves of this, but some people do it. It's very secluded on Tashangfang, where Master Su and his disciple moved. There are some caves up there.

Q: What about Loukuantai?

Hsueh: They don't have as many visitors as Huashan, but too many people live there. It's no good either. Their lives are too comfortable. If you want to find a place to practice, you have to go into the mountains. But if you do, food and clothes are a problem. Either you have to come out of the mountains to buy things, or you have to depend on others. This is the problem. But people who practice in the mountains have a way of dealing with this. They don't eat grain or wear clothes. Maybe they wear a few rags. They practice yoga so that they don't get hungry or cold. Most people, though, can't live in the mountains. It's not easy.

Q: How do people learn such cultivation?

Hsueh: You can learn the basics anywhere. There are books. As to

Master Hsueh: forty-five years on Huashan summit.

learning the inner secrets, when your practice reaches a certain level, you'll meet a teacher. But you can't be in a hurry. You have to be prepared to devote your whole life to your practice. This is what's meant by religion. It's not a matter of spending money. You have to spend your life. Not many people are willing to do this. If you're ready to learn, you don't have to look for a teacher. A teacher will find you. Taoism is very deep. There's a great deal to learn, and you can't do it quickly. The Tao isn't something that can be put into words. You have to practice before you can understand. Lao-tzu teaches us to be natural. You can't force things, including practice. Understanding is something that happens naturally. It's different for everyone. The main thing is to reduce your desires and quiet your mind. Practice takes a long time, and you have to stay healthy. If you have a lot of thoughts and desires, you won't live long enough to reach the end.

I liked Master Hsueh. He was straightforward in a very gentle way, and I could have talked to him for hours. But it was already noon, and several other visitors had arrived. Later, I read in the Taoist association magazine that Hsueh had recently given all the money he had saved from donations over the past forty years, amounting to 2,000 RMB, or about four hundred dollars, to the association for the construction of new temples.

As Steve and I got up to leave, Master Hsueh went into his bedroom. He came back out with a bag of pine seeds that he had collected from trees that grew at the summit. Huashan pines are a special species native to the summits of the higher peaks of the Chungnan Mountains. They're famous among tree growers throughout China, Korea, and Japan, and those that grow on Huashan's West Peak are the most famous of all. Their seeds, pollen, and even their needles were a staple in the diet of Taoists who lived on Huashan in the past. Ancient texts claim that after a thousand years the resin from the Huashan pine turns into amber and that eating it can transform a person into an immortal. Master Hsueh said to eat the seeds or plant them and grow trees. I told him I was an old friend of the pine family and would rather grow trees.

We didn't linger. Two hours later I stopped to wait for Steve at Chunhsien Temple. Master Hsieh had been the abbot of this temple before his legs became arthritic. It had been built in 1919 by Hsieh's master and was empty except for one young Taoist monk serving lunch to a group of visitors. While I rested on the steps, the monk came out and we talked. He said young Taoists were in a fix. All they did was take care of tourists. He said that most masters taught the inner secrets to only one disciple during their lifetime and that the great masters had gone deeper into the mountains, refusing to teach in this material age. He said instruction in the temples was superficial. He sighed, then went back inside to finish serving lunch.

After Steve arrived, we continued down the trail together. Along the way, we passed a boulder with the words *ho-chih-sheng* ("sound of the crane") carved into its face and painted red. The crane is the Taoist symbol for transformation and transcendence, for detachment and purity, for long life. It was the perfect symbol for Huashan, but apparently the crane had flown off.

When the Buddhist travel-diarist Kao Ho-nien visited the mountain in 1904, he marveled at how the Taoists on Huashan were able to get by on so little. He also commented on the serenity of Huashan and the dedication to seclusion of those who lived here. He said this was not true for other Taoist mountains—and he had visited them all. Visiting Huashan at the other end of the twentieth century, I had to wonder why any Taoists would still want to live on the mountain. Its scenery, however impressive, was a poor substitute for solitude.

On the way down, we rested again at Shaloping. I remembered what Master Hsueh had said about Master Su moving with a disciple to a cave on the summit of Tashangfang. Tashangfang was somewhere up there in the clouds. I looked at the cliff across the gorge and wondered out loud how far up it was to Master Su's cave. A man who was selling slices of watermelon said he knew Master Su. He said Tashangfang wasn't far, and he offered to guide us.

We accepted his offer and followed him across the stream. On the other side, he showed us where the trail began. We stared in disbelief.

The trailhead was an iron chain hanging about thirty meters down the face of the cliff. Our guide pulled himself up, then waved for us to follow. Steve and I looked at each other with dismay, but what respectable excuse could we offer? So we followed. The next part was even more frightening: finger and toe holds up a seventy-degree slope made slick by a seeping spring. And no chain. Terrified to look down, we just kept climbing so that we wouldn't think about the drop.

After about a hundred meters, we reached the ruins of an ancient hermitage, then started up an even steeper cliff. Halfway up, legs wobbling from exhaustion and fright, I asked our guide how much farther it was. He said two hours and pointed to the top of a cliff just below the clouds. When he'd told us Master Su's cave "wasn't far," I had neglected to ask him what that meant. Now that I knew, I realized we couldn't possibly make it. We had less than two hours of daylight and practically no strength. We decided to visit Master Su another day, and descended slowly to the main trail.

Walking on flat ground was such a thrill, Steve started skipping down the trail. As he passed other people on their way down, they started skipping too. Soon there were about a dozen Chinese skipping behind a foreigner who looked a lot like Rip van Winkle. That night my sides hurt from laughing. A week later, my legs finally stopped hurting.

*T*hat should have been the end of this chapter, but seven months later I visited Huashan again. It was late March, and everything had changed. There was almost no water in the stream, and the walls of the gorge were sere, except for an occasional wild peach tree in bloom. When I reached Shaloping, I stopped to talk with our former guide. He said Master Su and his disciple had come down from Tashangfang for a few days and were staying at Chaoyuantung Temple at the mouth of the gorge. I smiled, happy in the thought that I wouldn't have to climb that cliff again, and returned to Jade Spring Temple.

In the courtyard, I saw a nun who looked unusually serene and asked her the way to Chaoyuantung. She led me to a gate along the west wall and pointed toward a bamboo grove in the distance. Beyond the gate, I worked my way back to the mouth of the gorge, crossed the stream, and walked along an irrigation ditch. After about two hundred meters, I entered the bamboo grove that hid Chaoyuantung from view. This was where Ho Yuan-hsi lived when he first came to Huashan in the thirteenth century, before he carved out his cave on South Peak.

The temple consisted of several old adobe buildings with thatched roofs. I patted the two stone lions near the entrance and went inside. Despite its dilapidated condition, the place was filled with monks and laymen. I approached an old monk who turned out to be the abbot. I told him I was looking for Master Su and asked him what was going on. He said Master Su and his disciple were staying at Shihertung on the other side of Jade Spring Temple and that monks and nuns from all over the province had come to Huashan to take part in three days of ceremonies marking the third anniversary of the death of Master Ts'ao's mother. Master Ts'ao was the head of the Huashan Taoist Association and was, I learned later, the nun who had pointed me in the direction of Chaoyuantung.

I returned to Jade Spring Temple and headed toward Shihertung. As I walked across the grounds, I ran into old Master Hsueh. On West Peak, he lived alone. Here, at the bottom of the mountain, he was surrounded by a dozen young disciples. We greeted each other, and he said he had just returned from Peking where he had taken part in the first formal ceremonies held since 1949 ordaining new Taoist monks and nuns. He asked me if I had planted the pine seeds. I told him I had given them to friends of the forests of Taiwan, Japan, and America. When I asked him about Master Su, he disappeared into what looked like a temporary mess tent and returned with a tall monk who looked about forty.

Hsueh introduced the monk as Su's disciple. His name was Chou. When I said I had tried to visit him and his master the previous fall, he said if I waited another year or two I might have an easier climb. Taiwan's Tien Ti Association, he said, had offered to finance construction of a safer trail. It was obvious he didn't welcome the offer. Just then, another monk came out of the tent. Chou said this was Master Su. I bowed and introduced myself. Without pausing, Su said I had the wrong man, that his name was Hua, as in Huashan. Then he walked off, flapping his long sleeves as if he were about to fly away.

Chapter Six

Road to
Heaven

*W*hen Buddhism first reached China two thousand years ago, it was already half-Chinese. Up until then, all major systems of thought and practice in China that could be called religious were based on an understanding of the Tao. Since the Tao was sufficiently fertile to have given birth to all of creation, there was no reason to think another system couldn't be derived from its womb. And for at least a hundred years after it first appeared, Buddhism caused few conceptual problems for the Chinese.

China's first encounters with the Dharma, or Buddhist view of reality, occurred no later than the first century B.C., when the Han dynasty established its influence along a necklace of oases stretching all the way to the kingdoms of northwest India, where Mahayana Buddhism was just emerging. The first contacts were diplomatic. Diplomatic contacts, though, would have never resulted in the introduction of Buddhism, except as a curiosity. It was commerce that brought the Dharma to China in the caravans of merchants who came to trade incense, precious gems, and colored glass for Chinese silk. Merchants from Central Asia were living in permanent communities outside the walls of China's political centers as early as the first century A.D., and living with them were Buddhist monks from India.

Details of Buddhism's introduction to the Chinese are likely to remain unknown. Documents and artifacts only tell us that it didn't take long for the Buddha to be accepted as another god in the growing Taoist religion, which now included such utopian movements as the Yellow Turbans. By the second century, the Buddha was not only being worshipped alongside Lao-tzu, he had become sufficiently popular with some Taoists to be considered Lao-tzu himself. Lao-tzu, after all, was said to have headed west after leaving Loukuantai, and a book appeared in the second century recounting the sage's disappearance from China and reappearance in India as the Buddha. In his *Essay on Taoism in the First Centuries A.D.* (in *Taoism and Chinese Religion* [Amherst: University of Massachusetts Press, 1981]), Henri Maspero explains why Taoists so readily believed such stories and welcomed the Enlightened One to China:

> Buddhism was considered a particular Taoist sect, the strictest of them, more balanced and more reasonable than the Yellow Turbans. Moreover, it had the advantage of avoiding alchemical practices and of being a purely moral and contemplative method of immortality. This set it apart and gave it a luster which the small number of its adherents and its foreign character would otherwise not have allowed it to hope for. This new sect joined up with the old mystical masters of Taoism, Lao-tzu and Chuang-tzu, and from certain points of view came closer to them than the Taoism of the time. (P. 411)

But such rapport was not to last. Increasing interest in this Taoism from what the Chinese called the Western Regions soon resulted in translations of Buddhist texts that by the end of the second century revealed fundamental differences in doctrine and practice. While Taoists sought to create a deathless body, Buddhists sought liberation from all bodies. Nirvana, it turned out, was not the same as the Taoist goal of immortality. Meditation practices differed too. Taoists reduced their breathing to the barest minimum and concentrated on the circulation and transformation of the body's inner breath, while Buddhists emphasized regulated breathing and detachment from the workings of the body. Also, Buddhists recognized a commonly held set of rules, or precepts, by which to regulate their conduct, while Taoists, for the most part, pointed themselves in the direction of virtue and otherwise left each other to their own devices. By the third century, Buddhism was on its own, as Taoists either became converts or rejected what was now branded a foreign faith.

Over the following centuries, Buddhism not only flourished in its new setting, it became sufficiently mature to develop new schools of thought and practice, which further extended its appeal to the Chinese. As with Taoism, the Chungnan Mountains formed the backdrop to the emergence and development of this new religious tradition. Of the eight major Buddhist schools that flowered in China, seven of them shed their first petals in or near the Chungnan Mountains. These were the Three Treatise, Mind-Only, Precept, Pure Land, Huayen, Tantric, and Zen schools, the last of which reportedly began on Sungshan, an eastern spur of the Chungnan Mountains. The eighth major school was the Tientai school, which began on Hengshan and Tientaishan in southern and eastern China.

Of these eight ways of looking at the Dharma, none was more important in terms of influence or number of adherents than the Pure Land school. Instead of teaching people that liberation depended solely on their own effort, the Pure Land doctrine taught faith in the power of Amita Buddha to bring devotees to his paradise, where liberation was more easily attained than in this world of impurity. The means whereby such faith availed itself of this buddha's power included the chanting of Amita's name, the visualization of his paradise, and the vow to be reborn there.

The establishment of this doctrine in China and the popularization of these practices are attributed to Shan-tao, whose name I first learned when I arrived in Taiwan almost twenty years ago. The monks at the Buddhist temple where I spent my first year on the island asked me to translate a Buddhist sutra, or sermon of the Buddha. Despite being new to the language of the sutras, I was grateful to them for providing me with free room and board, and I tried to oblige.

Out of curiosity, I picked one of the Pure Land school's major scriptures: the sutra in which the Buddha instructs Queen Vaidehi in a series
of sixteen visualizations that begins with the setting sun on the western
horizon and proceeds to an expanse of water that turns into a plain of
aquamarine on which appears a land of gardens, palaces, and pavilions
decked with colored lights and jewels. All the sounds in this land, including those of birds, trees, and water, chant the words *suffering,
emptiness, impermanence,* and *selflessness.* This is the Western Paradise, Sukhavati, the Pure Land, the Land of Amita Buddha, the Buddha of Infinite Light and Infinite Life, before whom Vaidehi finally sees
herself reappear from out of a lotus flower. The Buddha tells Vaidehi
that anyone able to visualize this land and its buddha is a white lotus
among mankind and destined to be reborn in this paradise.

Shan-tao read this sutra soon after he became a monk in A.D. 631
and was so overcome by it that he moved from eastern China to the
Chungnan Mountains and practiced these visualizations for several
years. Despite his devotion, he still harbored doubts about the basis
for such practice. In 641, he traveled north to Hsuanchung Temple
near Taiyuan to study with Tao-ch'o. As the spiritual heir of T'an-
luan, an earlier abbot of the temple, Tao-ch'o had already gained a
reputation as a teacher of Pure Land practice. He convinced Shan-tao
of the importance of chanting the name of Amita Buddha; such practice, he said, was sufficient in itself to guarantee rebirth in the Pure
Land.

After Tao-ch'o's death in 645, Shan-tao returned to the Chungnan
Mountains and the sanctuary of Wuchen Temple. The temple had
been built about fifty years earlier and included two groups of buildings, one of them at the mouth of Wuchen Gorge and the other nearly
two kilometers inside the gorge. When the poet-official Pai Chu-yi
moved to this area in 811 to spend the three-year mourning period for
his mother, he wrote a 260-line poem entitled "Visiting Wuchen
Temple." The poem speaks of the majesty of the surrounding mountains and the splendor of the buildings, which housed over a thousand
monks and nuns.

Steve and I wanted to see what was left of the splendor, so we hired a car and driver. From Sian, we drove fifty kilometers southeast to Lantien. Another five kilometers east of town, we turned south on a rutted, dirt road and soon came to the new gray wall that surrounded Shuilu Convent. The convent had been built a century or two before Wuchen Temple and was later included as part of the temple complex. As its name indicates, it was once used as a residence for nuns. Foreign affairs police in Sian told us Wuchen Temple was off-limits, but they couldn't make up their minds about Shuilu Convent.

We soon discovered the place was being run by party cadres. At first, they insisted foreigners weren't allowed. But after much persuasion from the monk who had accompanied us, they finally agreed to let us inside for a quick look around. The statuary in the main shrine hall included an incredible display of several thousand clay figures, most of which had been fashioned in the early fifteenth century. It was among the most impressive artwork we'd seen anywhere in China, but after a few minutes the caretakers became nervous and hurried us out the main gate.

While Steve was stowing his gear, I talked with two old women at the temple entrance. They were selling *ling-chih,* a type of fungus found on the shady side of trees and cliffs. Taoists include it in most of their recipes for immortality. Since *ling-chih* meant immortals, and immortals meant hermits, I asked the old women if there were any cultivators of the Way in the area. Without stopping to think, much less count, one of them said there were more than seventy living within a day's hike of Wangshunshan, whose 2,300-meter peak rose ten kilometers to the southeast past the end of the gorge. Despite their ancient appearance, the women said they hiked up Wangshunshan and other nearby mountains several times a week to look for herbs.

I was about to ask about the hermits and trails around Wangshunshan, but the man in charge of the temple insisted we leave immediately. As we drove off, our driver told us to make ourselves invisible. Foreigners, it turned out, weren't allowed in the area due to the presence of a uranium mine at the mouth of the gorge. Apparently, the caretakers of the temple were under the impression that Steve had included the mine in the background of several panoramic shots. We crouched down and only resurfaced when we entered Lantien. We had to laugh. In ancient times, the Lantien area was famous for jade, a mineral Taoists used in their quest for immortality. Now it was uranium. Two different minerals, two dead ends on the road to heaven.

After five years of listening to the Wuchen River chant the Dharma, Shan-tao left the Lantien area and moved to the nearby outskirts of Ch'ang-an, where he spent most of his remaining years preaching and painting pictures of the Pure Land.

In 681, he left for the Pure Land himself, and his disciples built a pagoda south of Chang'an to house his remains. A monastic community soon developed there, and it became the first center of the new Pure Land school. It was called Hsiangchi Temple. In Japan, where the Pure Land sect claims more than 50 million members, schoolchildren still memorize a poem written in the eighth century by Wang Wei:

> *unaware of Hsiangchi Temple*
> *walking for miles in the clouds*
> *ancient trees an empty path*
> *somewhere in the hills a bell*
> *streamsound murmuring boulders*
> *sunshine cold green pines*
> *fading light a silent pool*
> *zen to tame the serpent*

In March, six months after Steve and I were chased away from Shan-tao's former retreat, I returned to Sian alone and resumed my travels. The road led me seventeen kilometers south of Sian, through the Ch'ang-an county seat, past two police checks, up and across Shenho Plateau, through the village of Chialitsun, then west on a side road to the adobe walls of Hsiangchi Temple, surrounded now by farmland.

Inside, I met the temple's sixty-eight-year-old abbot, Hsu-tung. He showed me around and talked about the temple's recent history. When he first came here in 1960, the only structures still standing were one shrine hall and three pagodas containing the remains of

Hsu-tung, with Shan-tao's pagoda in the background.

Shan-tao and two later Pure Land masters. There was only one old monk then, and the two of them lived in a small thatched hut next to the shrine hall. By 1963, there were nineteen monks. Then, in the late sixties, the Red Guards came and reduced one of the pagodas to rubble and forced the monks to join local work crews. Somehow Hsu-tung managed to save the shrine hall and the remaining two pagodas.

Despite such a difficult beginning, Hsu-tung has now almost completed the work of restoration, at least on a rudimentary level. Once the primary school occupying the front courtyard moves to a new location, the temple grounds will amount to nearly two hectares, or about one-fifth of their former size. New quarters for the monks are also under construction. Even though the government has restricted the number that can register at the temple to fifteen, nearly thirty monks were living there when I visited.

Hsu-tung led me to Shan-tao's thirty-two-meter pagoda, and I lit some incense in the small shrine inside the base. I would have liked to see the view from the top, but the stairs had become too dangerous, and there was a gate barring access.

Hsu-tung next took me through the temple's vegetable gardens. It was late March, and the monks were just beginning to plant cabbages, eggplants, red peppers, and potatoes. Hsu-tung said the temple did not buy food.

The paths were lined with rosebushes. I thought of the rose as a Western flower and was always surprised to see it in China. But a botanist in Sian assured me that the rose was first cultivated in Ch'ang-an two thousand years ago from a wild variety native to the Chungnan Mountains. Like marijuana thousands of years earlier, it eventually traveled the Silk Road to India, the Mediterranean, and beyond.

Near the main shrine hall, there were several banana trees, which also seemed out of place. When I asked Hsu-tung if it wasn't too cold for them to bear fruit, he said he planted them just for fun. I nodded. I planted one outside my window in Taiwan, also just for fun, for the sound of summer rain. I lit more incense in the temple's two renovated shrine halls, then joined Hsu-tung in his room for a cup of tea. I noticed he was missing the tip of one finger. I wondered if he had burnt it as an offering to Amita Buddha, a not uncommon practice in the past — one of the most famous poets of the Ch'ing dynasty was a monk known as Eight Fingers.

Before Hsu-tung moved to China's most famous Pure Land temple, he had been the abbot of Tamaopeng Hermitage, the most renowned Zen temple in the Chungnan Mountains. I asked him about the difference between Zen and Pure Land practice.

Hsu-tung: In Zen, we keep asking who's chanting the name of the Buddha. All we think about is where the name of the Buddha is coming from. We keep asking, until we find out who we were before we were born. This is Zen. We sit with one mind. And if the mind runs off somewhere, we follow it wherever it goes, until the mind finally becomes quiet, until there's no Zen to Zen, no question to question, until we reach the stage where we question without questioning and without questioning we keep questioning. We keep questioning, until we finally find an answer, until delusions come to an end, until we can swallow the world, all its rivers and mountains, everything, but the world can't swallow us, until we can ride the tiger, but the tiger can't ride us, until we find out who we really are. This is Zen.

In Pure Land practice, we just chant the name of the Buddha, nothing more. We chant with the mind. We chant without making a sound, and yet the sound is perfectly clear. And when we hear the sound, the chant begins again. It goes around and around. The chant doesn't stop, and the mind doesn't move. The sound arises, we hear the sound, but our mind doesn't move. And when our mind doesn't move, delusions disappear. And once they're gone, the one mind chants. The result is the same as Zen. Zen means no distinctions. Actually, Pure Land practice includes Zen, and Zen practice includes Pure Land practice. If you don't practice both, you become one-sided.

Q: Is Pure Land practice more appropriate for the present age?

Hsu-tung: All practices are appropriate. There's no right or wrong dharma. It's a matter of aptitude, your connections from past lives.

Once people start practicing, they think other kinds of practice are wrong. But all practices are right. It depends on the individual as to which is more appropriate.

And all practices are related. They involve each other. They lead to the same end. Pure Land practice, for example, includes the precepts. You can't chant the name of the Buddha without leading an upright life. And Pure Land practice includes Zen. You can't chant the name of the Buddha unless you chant with one mind. It's the same as Zen. The goal is the same. Practice is like candy. People like different kinds. But it's just candy. The Dharma is empty.

Q: What's so special about the Chungnan Mountains? Why do so many people come here to practice?

Hsu-tung: The Chungnan Mountains stretch all the way to India. When the first monks came to China, they settled in these mountains. And most of the great monks and nuns in China practiced here. But that was in the past. The reason so many monks and nuns still come to these mountains is that it's still easy to find a secluded place. Also, there are still plenty of lay people in this area willing to help support those who come to practice.

Q: How many hermits are living in these mountains now?

Hsu-tung: I'd say about fifty in Ch'ang-an County and two hundred in the mountains between Lantien and Paochi. But it's been a while since I was in the mountains, so there might be more. Monks and nuns who live in the mountains don't have to register with anyone, so there's no way of knowing.

The only way of knowing was to enter the mountains. I said good-bye to Hsu-tung, but on my way back to the parking lot, I walked down to where the Hao and the Chueh rivers met to become the Chiao River about two hundred meters southwest of the temple. Village men were shoveling gravel from the banks into donkey carts. Women were pounding clothes on boulders. The summer rains hadn't begun, and both rivers were only about twenty meters wide. A few people had taken off their shoes and were wading across. Two thousand years ago, the plain to the south was an imperial forest, planted with chestnut and pear trees. In the distance, I could see orchards. In nearby fields, farmers were sitting on short stools pulling weeds out of new millet.

Back on the highway, we continued south. The road was paved, but there wasn't much traffic. At one point, we passed an old woman sitting in the middle of the road leisurely sewing a pair of pants. After eight kilometers, the road ended at the village of Tzuwu and the entrance to the ancient trail that armies once used when crossing the mountains. We turned west.

After ten kilometers, we reached the village of Fengyukou, situated at the entrance to the road that has replaced the Tzuwu Trail, connecting Sian with the southern side of the Chinling Range. A police check caught my driver with expired insurance. Car insurance costs around 800 RMB per year. The police check cost 20 RMB, about four dollars. We continued heading west, skirting the mountains. Eight kilometers later, just past the munitions plant in Kaokuan Gorge, we turned north and shortly afterward arrived at Tsaotang Temple. This was where I came with Steve in May of 1989 on the Buddha's Birthday during my first trip to the Chungnan Mountains.

In the courtyard, Abbot Hung-lin welcomed me back and unlocked the door to Kumarajiva's stupa so that I could pay my respects again. It was Kumarajiva who led me here in the first place. His shrine was a simple brick pavilion with nothing inside except three meters of beautifully carved marble. I imagined him sitting inside working on a translation of another Buddhist sutra. Records say that when he was cremated in A.D. 413 his tongue didn't burn.

Kumarajiva was born sixty-nine years earlier, in 344, in the Silk Road kingdom of Kucha. By the time he was thirty, he was instructing rulers of the region in the Dharma, and travelers on the Silk Road were carrying stories about him to Ch'ang-an. To establish Chinese rule farther into the Western Regions, Emperor Fu Chien sent General Lu Kuang in 382 with an army of seventy thousand soldiers to subdue Kucha and escort Kumarajiva back to the capital. After completing the first part of his mission, Lu Kuang learned that there had been a change in dynasties. Instead of returning to Ch'ang-an, he stopped in the Kansu Corridor. He established his own kingdom at Liangchou and detained Kumarajiva there for seventeen years, until he himself was defeated by Emperor Yao Hsing.

When Kumarajiva finally arrived in Ch'ang-an in 401, Yao Hsing invited him to live in the Hsiaoyao Garden, between the northern wall of the palace and the Wei River. Such was the emperor's respect for Kumarajiva's abilities, he gave him the title of National Preceptor and placed three thousand monks and scholars at his disposal to help him in his translation work. The emperor often took part as well, holding versions of previous translations for Kumarajiva to compare. Living so close to the capital, however, was distracting for Kumarajiva. Also distracting was the emperor's request that the monk divide his nights among ten ladies of the court in hopes of transmitting his genius to future generations. Apparently Kumarajiva acquiesced in this eugenic experiment. He prefaced his sermons by telling his listeners to take only the lotus and not to touch the mud from which it grew.

After four years, Kumarajiva moved to the relative quiet of Tsaotang Temple, where he spent most of his remaining years. The original temple had been built as a family shrine sometime during the previous century and was called Tashih Temple. Following Kumarajiva's arrival, it was expanded to accommodate his retinue of assistants and renamed Tsaotang, or Hall of Thatch. It was clearly a misnomer, but it seemed appropriate as it was in the shadow of the Chungnan Mountains.

Regardless of where he worked, Kumarajiva produced translations that sixteen hundred years later remain unsurpassed in both style and phrasing. His *Vimilakirti Sutra* is considered one of the gems of Chinese literature, and his *Diamond Sutra* and *Heart Sutra* are probably the most quoted Buddhist texts in China. His translations also contained more music than those of other translators. To this day, it's impossible to get through a Buddhist ceremony anywhere in the Orient without Kumarajiva's help. His *Amitabha Sutra* is among the basic texts of the Pure Land school; his *Lotus Sutra* inspired formation of the Tientai school; and his translations of the works of Nagarjuna and

Aryadeva became the basic texts of the Three Treatise school founded by his own disciples.

Abbot Hung-lin relocked the pavilion that housed Kumarajiva's stupa, then led me past a bamboo grove to one of the province's eight wonders, a well from which vapor is said to rise in autumn and drift all the way to Sian. Autumn, though, was six months away, and the only thing I noticed was Hung-lin's shy smile. Nearby, Hung-lin also showed me a large, empty pond, with new stone walls and a new stone bridge and pavilion. He said every April several feet of water seeped into the pond from an underground source and provided a place to plant aquatic vegetables. Apparently the well and pond are connected.

On the way back to the parking lot, we stopped in the courtyard. The ground was covered with cedar fronds drying in the sun. Hung-lin said the monks made their own incense and sold it to pilgrims for use in the shrine hall. The dozen or so monks who lived at the temple used the money to buy building materials and the few things they couldn't make. They didn't have to buy food. The walls enclosed two hectares of good farm land.

Hung-lin remembered that I was interested in visiting hermits, and he pointed toward Kueifeng's distinctive pyramid-shaped peak several kilometers to the southwest at the mouth of Taiping Gorge. He said he had lived in a hut on Kueifeng for several years himself. He was seventy-three and had been a monk since he was eighteen. He asked me if I would like to meet a ninety-four-year-old monk who was living near his old hut just below the summit. I was ready to accept his offer, but when he added that the monk had lost the power of speech and that arrangements would have to be made with the military commander at the foot of the mountain, I decided to decline.

The name Kueifeng, though, was one I knew. It was the posthumous name of Tsung-mi, who served as abbot of Tsaotang Temple in the ninth century and was a patriarch of both the Huayen school and a branch of the Zen school. When we left the courtyard, Hung-lin stopped and unlocked the drum tower. Inside was Tsung-mi's grave stele. Its inscription had been composed and written by Pei Hsiu, the ninth-century prime minister who recorded the sermons of several famous Zen masters, including those of Huang-po. I thanked Hung-lin for his help and told him I would rather be in the mountains. He smiled shyly, and we said good-bye.

On my way back to Fengyukou, I stopped a short distance south of Tsaotang Temple beside a vineyard. With the help of a farmer, I found what I was looking for on the west side of the road: the former site of Hsingfu Stupa Cemetery. The cemetery had once included Tsung-mi's Blue Lotus Stupa along with those of more than fifty other eminent monks. The stone and brick structures were destroyed during the Cultural Revolution, and the site was now a large depression in a large vineyard. Local officials, I'd heard, were planning to begin digging for relics to enshrine as future tourist attractions. The farmer said he had heard the same thing, but he was still taking good care of his vines.

A few minutes later, I was back in the village of Fengyukou. On the east side of the entrance to the Feng River gorge, I climbed up the base of Houanshan through a leafless forest illuminated by wild peach trees. Soon I reached a small plateau dominated by the new red walls and gray-tiled roofs of Fengte Temple. The temple was one of several associated with Tao-hsuan, who lived on this mountain in the middle of the seventh century.

The temple had seen better days, its new walls notwithstanding. Still, life goes on. Inside, I heard the sound of a pedal-operated sewing machine, and I saw irises and a cherry tree in bloom. The monastery was now a nunnery. Outside, I met the abbess, Miao-chueh. She was sixty years old and from Heilungkiang Province in the northeast. She was busy picking vegetables near the former graveyard where three stone stupas still leaned. She stopped long enough to tell me that more than thirty nuns were living at the temple, but she didn't know how long it had been a nunnery. It was still a monastery in the ninth century when Tsung-mi lived here and wrote his classic essay on the varieties of Zen.

I returned to the village and entered the gorge: high rocky cliffs on both sides of a winding, clear river and a paved road along its eastern edge. After less than two kilometers, I stopped at a place called Liulin-ping. The first time I came here I was with Steve. But Steve was back in America, and I started up the new stone steps that led up the mountain alone. Far above, on the summit of Houanshan, I could see Tao-hsuan's stupa, which had led us here the year before on the Buddha's Birthday.

Halfway up, I stopped at Chingyeh Temple. Over the temple's main door I saw the words that greeted me the first time I came here: "Use the Dharma to protect the Dharma." The temple dog barked. One of the monks came out and led me inside. He told me the dog was making up for one rainy night several months earlier when he had slept while someone sneaked in over the walls. The intruder had stripped the bark from two tu-chung trees (*Eucommia ulmoides*) to sell for its medicinal value. The trees were now dead. They had been planted in the temple's small courtyard more than thirteen hundred years ago by Tao-hsuan.

Tao-hsuan was the founder of the Precept school, and Chingyeh Temple was the school's center. When Tao-hsuan first came here in 621 at the age of twenty-five, he lived in a hut farther up the mountain. Later, he moved down to the temple, which had been built fifty years before his arrival. As the number of his disciples grew, he used the temple as an instruction center and a supply base for those who stayed in nearby huts on the mountain. In addition to compiling biographies of early Buddhist monks in China, he devoted himself to standardizing the rules under which monks and nuns regulated their lives, and he used these rules, or precepts, as the basis for religious instruction. Although this school has never been prominent, it still has its adherents, and monks and nuns of other schools follow its dictum that nothing can be accomplished without leading an upright life.

When Steve and I visited Chingyeh Temple the previous August, we met K'uan-ming, a twenty-eight-year-old monk who had been put in charge of overseeing the temple's restoration. During that visit I asked him if there were still precept masters in China.

K'uan-ming: At the end of the Ch'ing dynasty, there were En-yeh and Hung-yi. Nowadays there's Meng-san at the City of Ten Thousand

Tao-hsuan's stupa.

Buddhas in America, Yuan-chou at Kuanghua Temple in Putien [Fukien], Miao-tsan at Nanputuo in Hsiamen [Fukien], and the nun T'ung-nien in Chienhsien [100 kilometers northwest of Fengyukou]. These are the only precept masters I know of. They've all been helping finance restoration of Chingyeh Temple. They all say it's time for the Chungnan Mountains to begin training great monks and nuns again.

Q: What brought you here?

K'uan-ming: Monks and nuns are the freest people in China. We can go anywhere we want. Before the Cultural Revolution, we had to have a household registration. Now only those who live in a temple for a long time have to register. We're always moving from place to place to practice and learn. After studying at the Buddhist academy in Hsiamen, I came here to practice. That was three years ago. When I got off the bus, all I had was 120 RMB [about twenty-five dollars]. I used the money to build a hut on Kuanyinshan. After a month, I came here to pay my respects, and I met two old monks. We must have had a connection from some previous life. I stayed. Later, I went back to Hsiamen to see Master Meng, and he agreed to finance restoration of the temple into a place of practice.

Q: How many monks and nuns are living in these mountains?

K'uan-ming: Since I arrived, I've done a lot of hiking around. In Ch'ang-an County alone there must be more than five hundred. But there are two kinds. Most come to the mountains to practice. But there are some — how shall I say? — who take care of shrines and temples to keep themselves fed.

Q: How much longer do you plan to live here?

K'uan-ming: Another two or three years, until this temple is restored. Then I'd like to turn it over to someone who understands the Tao and who can revive the practice of the Precept school. After that, I'd like to spend a few years studying with Master Meng or Master Miao. Master Meng wants me to join him in America.

Q: Could you tell me about Master Meng?

K'uan-ming: He's from Heilungkiang Province, the same as me. He was already well known when he was in his thirties, and he lectured in Burma and Thailand as well as in Hong Kong. When he returned, he was imprisoned as a spy. They said he traveled too much. He spent more than thirty years in jail and was finally released in 1980. He's seventy-eight now. When I first met him at the Buddhist academy in Hsiamen, hundreds of ordinary people, not just monks and nuns, came to hear his lectures. He's a very powerful speaker, and his words are very deep. Recently, he traveled to America to lecture to Chinese audiences, and they've asked him to stay. He taught me a lot. So did Master Miao. Master Miao doesn't say much, but whatever he says is profound. He was once the abbot of the most famous Zen temple in China, Kaoming Temple in Yangchou. Both of them are enlightened masters.

Q: Can a person become enlightened without observing the precepts?

K'uan-ming: No. If you don't observe precepts, regardless of whether it's one precept or two hundred and fifty [the number monks agree to live by], your life won't have any peace. When you observe precepts, you get rid of obstacles and attachments. And only then does your meditation become deeper. And only through meditation do you achieve enlightenment. This is the reasoning behind the Precept school.

Q: What hopes do you see for a revival of Buddhism in China?

K'uan-ming: Things have changed a lot over the past ten years. In Shensi Province there's hardly a village without some kind of temple or shrine for worshipers to go to. And worshipers are from all walks of life, including the government and the party. All that we need are some great masters. But for now, our main role seems to be to refamiliarize people with Buddhism. Of course, a lot of temples have become zoos, and the monks are treated like animals. People just come to look, and they make a lot of noise. But we think this will change, and temples will become places of worship and practice again. But this will take time. By then the old monks will be gone. So the future depends on us. We have to practice hard. That's why we don't sell tickets here. We're not a zoo. We don't let people inside, unless they're here to worship. But we still need money to fix up the temple, so I've started the monks making agate rosaries. Eventually, I think we can support ourselves from this.

Q: What about other temples?

K'uan-ming: They're the same. If they don't find a way to support themselves through their own effort or from donations, they have to rely on selling tickets to visitors. We're all well aware of the consequences of this. The great masters are already very old and have not been allowed to teach until recently. Unless the new generation of monks and nuns is diligent, there will be nothing left of this religion. Even though we have religious freedom now, every year things get worse. Conditions were better ten years ago when restrictions on religion were first lifted. Since then, it's become clear that the government wants to turn temples into tourist centers.

It was six months later, and K'uan-ming had returned to Hsiamen in Fukien Province. Apparently, he was preparing to join Meng-san in America. He'd been replaced by K'ai-lung, another young monk and a graduate of the Chinese department of Peking University. In fact, among the eight or nine monks living at the temple, three were graduates of the university's Chinese department. At other Buddhist temples also, I was surprised by the high level of education among the young monks and nuns. When I was in Peking, I learned that the Buddhist association required all new monks and nuns to have at least a high school education. The Taoist association had no such requirement.

K'ai-lung led me into one of the three caves hollowed out behind the main shrine hall. It served as a dining room, and I was just in time for dinner: cornmeal mush, a wild vegetable, and fried potatoes. Afterward, K'ai-lung showed me to a room for the night. The next thing I remember is waking to the sounds of someone working the bellows of the kitchen stove, a woodpecker looking for grubs, and songbirds. Then someone struck the slotted log that hung near the kitchen. Breakfast was the same as dinner, except freshly made steamed buns replaced the fried potatoes.

During my previous visit, I had met a nun by the name of Yuan-chao on Kuanyinshan farther up the gorge. When I told K'ai-lung that I wanted to talk with her again, he said she had moved to the back side of the mountain and the trail was difficult. After breakfast, he talked to a young monk who had tried unsuccessfully to visit her the week before. Even though it was already mid-March, he hadn't been able to get through the snow. The weather, though, had been sunny all week, and he agreed to give the trail another try.

We hiked down to the paved road and started walking up the gorge. Several buses passed us by. The young monk said buses didn't usually stop unless they had to let someone off because it was too difficult to build up speed again. After a few minutes, we managed to hitch a ride in a truck, and fifteen kilometers later, we began hiking up the east slope of Kuanyinshan.

A hundred meters above the road, the trail led past a group of farm-houses, turned left at a pig sty, and began snaking up a steep slope that would have been impossible to climb if it had been wet or icy. Even dry, it was hard going, and I had to stop frequently to catch my breath. My companion must have wondered what I was doing in these mountains. I wondered myself. Finally, after ninety minutes, the trail leveled off, and we arrived at Shuilien Cave. This was where Yuan-chao had been living when I met her six months earlier. The cave's new occupant wasn't at home, and after lighting some incense in the cave shrine, we went on. Twenty minutes later, a stone archway announced Nanya Temple on a side trail to the left.

When I climbed Kuanyinshan with Steve and K'uan-ming the previous fall, we stayed on the main trail and ten minutes later reached the summit: a gateway of huge pines and a series of four or five shrines crowding the peak. In one shrine, we met a seventy-year-old Buddhist monk who had been ordained the previous year and who probably fell into K'uan-ming's rice-bowl hermit category. In another shrine, we saw a group of lay disciples receiving instruction in yoga from a young Taoist. But we stayed outside. K'uan-ming remarked that the weather was special, and we had to agree. The panorama of peaks and pines and clouds changed every few seconds. I smoked a whole cigar just sitting there watching, listening to my favorite song, the wind in the pines.

This time, I decided to bypass the peak, and we headed instead for Nanya Temple. A few minutes later, we were welcomed by Ch'ang-chao, the temple's abbot and its only monk. He was seventy-one and had lived at the temple for nine years. Two laymen lived with him. While one of them poured us bowls of hot sugar-water, the abbot displayed a small bell given to the temple by the emperor three hundred years ago at the beginning of the Ch'ing dynasty. It was rather crude and seemed to indicate that Nanya Temple had not been high on the emperor's list of temples. Outside, Ch'ang-chao showed us a new shrine hall that was nearing completion, and he pointed to Wanhuashan's 2,000-meter peak directly across from Kuanyinshan on the east side of the Feng River gorge. Several monks had recently built huts on Wanhuashan, he said, and others were planning to join them. He said it was much more secluded than Kuanyinshan. I made a note.

It was noon, but the abbot didn't invite us to stay for lunch. Apparently the temple's food supply was too low. We said good-bye and began heading down the other side of Kuanyinshan. There were still traces of snow, but one week of sun had made a big difference. Ten minutes later, we reached the small shrine of Hsiching Temple. A nun came out to greet us. She was a disciple of Yuan-chao and lived there by herself. She insisted we stay for some leftover fried rice. I think she must have been a southerner. Bread and noodles are the normal fare in the north. While she was busy heating up the rice, I looked around and noticed that, like Nanya Temple, Hsiching included a small, separate shrine for Taoist deities. Something for everyone.

After lunch, we continued down the trail. At one point, we startled a rabbit as big as a dog. The mountainside was covered with last fall's leaves, and the noise of the rabbit bounding down the slope startled us as much as we startled it. Twenty minutes later, we passed Chin-chan Temple. No one at home. A few minutes later, we passed a hut. Clothes drying in the sun were those of a nun. Again, no one at home. Five minutes later, we reached the bottom of a ravine, crossed a log bridge, and headed up the other side. After another couple of minutes, we arrived at Lungwang Temple. It was an old nunnery that dated back to the Ming dynasty. About a hundred meters to the southeast was the site of the future Kuanyin Temple. Looking back at Kuanyinshan, I estimated we were less than two kilometers southwest of the peak.

One of the nuns at Lungwang Temple told us that Yuan-chao was living in an adobe hut on a small plateau that had been leveled off for Kuanyin Temple's future shrine hall. We followed the nun up the slope to Yuan-chao's hut. She was sitting cross-legged on her *k'ang*, an adobe bed with a built-in oven common throughout northern China.

As I walked in, she said, "You're back. Good. Now we can talk. Last time I wasn't sure. Now I know you've come for the Dharma." I was glad I had made the effort to visit her again. She was eighty-eight, but I've seldom talked with anyone as alert. She was born in Chilin Province in northeast China into a family of six generations of doctors. Her grandfather was a Buddhist monk, and her father also became a monk. She became a novice at sixteen and graduated from the Buddhist academy in Peking. Afterward, she returned to the northeast, where she established four Buddhist academies. I asked her why she left northeast China and came to the Chungnan Mountains.

Yuan-chao: I was tricked. It was Chih-chen, that abbot of Wolung Temple in Sian, the one who chants the *Diamond Sutra* thirty times every day. He came to visit me in 1953, and when I went to see him off at the train station, he shoved a ticket in my hand and put me on the train with him. I arrived in Sian with nothing, not even a change of clothes. He wanted me to stop working and to practice instead.

Later, I took over as abbess of Tsaotang Temple. When the Red Guards came, I told them to go away. I didn't let them in. If I had, they would have destroyed Kumarajiva's stupa. I was ready to die. That was a long time ago. Finally, temple life got to be too much for me, and I moved to Kuanyinshan. That was ten years ago. I thought it would be a good place to die. Last year, I decided the front side of Kuanyinshan wasn't quiet enough, too many people hiking to the peak, so I moved to the back side. People still visit me, though. Two weeks ago, several university students came up and spent a week with me studying the *Avatamsaka Sutra.*

Q: I understand you practice Tantric Buddhism?

Yuan-chao: Yes, but there aren't many of us left. Very few people practice Tantra anymore. I first studied in Peking with the sixtieth incarnation of Gung-ga Buddha, the head of the Red sect. It's not the same as the Yellow sect of the Dalai Lama and the Panchen Lama. The Tantric path is shorter and faster. I was in a hurry to die, so I studied the Tantric path. I'm still waiting to die, just waiting for the fire.

Q: Is Tantric practice similar to Pure Land practice?

Yuan-chao: Tantric practice is closer to Zen. It's the pinnacle of Zen. But it's not for ordinary people. It's like flying an airplane. It's dangerous. Pure Land practice is like driving an ox cart. It's safe. Anybody can do it. But it takes longer.

Yuan-chao had taught Buddhism to so many students for so many years, I think she had her lectures memorized, or at least her quotes, which she chanted. From my bag, I took out a sheet of calligraphy paper and asked if she would write down for me the essence of Buddhist practice. She put the paper aside, and I didn't raise the subject again. Two months later, back in Taiwan, I received the sheet of paper in the mail with four words: goodwill, compassion, joy, detachment. Her calligraphy was as strong and clear as her mind.

After dinner, my companion and I stretched out under blankets in an adobe hut across the future courtyard. In the middle of the night, the heavens rumbled, then exploded with one tremendous thunder-clap and poured rain until dawn.

When I went outside the next morning, I could hardly walk. A pound of sticky loess accumulated on my shoes with every step. After we finished our breakfast of cornmeal gruel and fried potatoes, Yuan-chao came over to our hut. She wanted to teach us a shortcut to en-lightenment that we could use if we were ever close to death. She said if we practiced it and weren't ready to die, we would get terrible headaches and die anyway. She chuckled as all three of us climbed un-

Yuan-chao on her k'ang, *waiting for the fire.*

der the blankets on our *k'ang,* and she taught us a mantra, a series of Sanskrit syllables, that she said had first been taught to mankind by beings from outer space. She also taught us another mantra that she said was an antidote, in case death decided to pass us by, or we it.

Afterward we walked outside. There was still some mist in the air, but the rain had stopped. We decided to go while we could. Yuan-chao said the trail over Kuanyinshan would be impossible and suggested a much easier and shorter route that led northwest along the side of a ravine down to the Feng River. The trail was covered with leaves, and the slope was gradual. She told us the county government had considered building a road up the ravine to develop the area for tourism but had put the plan on hold until the economy improved. We sighed at the thought, waved good-bye, and headed down the trail, practicing our new mantras along the way.

An hour later, we came out at the village of Weitzuping, crossed a bridge spanning the Feng River, which had turned wild during the night, and began walking down the road. Along the gorge were groves of bamboo; through the fog, wild peach. After an hour, we reached the village of Liyuanping. Another bridge took us back across the river.

We followed a trail through fields and past a huge pond at the southern end of the valley. Orange and golden fish darted around in the water. My companion said they were from Vietnam. Just past the pond, the trail to West Kuanyin Temple led straight up a steep slope, and it was slick. Fortunately, there were enough branches and rocks to hang onto along the way. An hour later, we crossed the saddle and headed down the other side. The trail leveled off. A yellow-crested woodpecker with black-and-white striped wings ignored us and continued to work on a snag. Somewhere in the fog, we reached the temple. We walked into the dirt courtyard, yelling the name of the Buddha. Four young monks and Abbot Sheng-lin appeared in the doorway. My companion drifted off to talk with the other monks, and the abbot invited me to join him in the kitchen. He said we could talk while he chopped kindling. He was seventy-four and had been a monk for over thirty years. For the past fourteen years, he had been living at West Kuanyin Temple. He had taken over from Ching-t'ien, who had moved to Chengtu in Szechuan Province to the south. When I asked Sheng-lin about his practice, he said he was too dumb to practice Zen, he just chanted the name of the Buddha. He laughed, but he wasn't joking.

Sheng-lin: Zen isn't suitable anymore. To practice Zen you need deep roots. People with deep roots are rare. They didn't used to be. In the past, anybody could practice Zen. But not now. This isn't just my opinion. It was Yin-kuang's opinion too. [Yin-kuang was a monk of the early twentieth century who reestablished Pure Land practice in China.] Nowadays, Pure Land practice is the only practice suitable for everyone. The difference is that Pure Land practice depends on the power of the Buddha. You don't need deep roots. Zen practice depends completely on yourself. It's much harder, especially now.

In the past, there were many enlightened monks. But how many are enlightened now? None that I know of. Some monks might think they're enlightened, but they're not. They mistake delusion for enlightenment. That's why Yin-kuang said it's better to chant the name of the Buddha, to rely on the Buddha. Who's more powerful, you or the Buddha? Pure Land practice is more certain to achieve results. If your roots aren't deep, and you practice Zen, you can practice all your life and never get anywhere. Pure Land practice isn't easy, though. You have to make up your mind to be reborn in the Pure Land; otherwise chanting the Buddha's name won't do any good, it's just superstition. Pure Land practice is beyond reason, it's a matter of faith. But faith is more powerful than reason. You can't see the Pure Land. Only buddhas can see the Pure Land. Eyes are useless. You have to rely on the Buddha.

Sheng-lin told me he was waiting for a great monk to take over the temple—he was just a caretaker. The temple could have passed for a farmhouse, but Sheng-lin said it was one of the best places in the Chungnan Mountains for practice. He said not even farmers came to this part of the mountains, and there was plenty of sunshine and water and good soil. Just before we had reached the temple, I had glimpsed part of the vegetable garden and a few fruit trees through the fog: he said their orchard included pear trees, apple trees, and persimmon trees. Then he laughed and related how the previous fall a bear had chased him and the other monks inside and had proceeded to eat half the temple's persimmon harvest, which had been drying outside. Sheng-lin didn't take himself very seriously. In one breath he rattled off the names of the first thirteen patriarchs of the Pure Land school, then laughed that he still remembered their names.

While I was talking with Sheng-lin, my young companion-guide came in and said it was time to go. It was midafternoon, and the only meal on the horizon was the one we would miss at Chingyeh Temple if we didn't leave right away.

On the way back, my guide told me that he and one of the young monks at West Kuanyin had lived together at Shaolin Temple. (Shaolin was the temple in Honan Province where Bodhidharma introduced the Chinese to Zen, and some say to martial arts as well.) He said the reputation of Shaolin monks was so bad that those who left had trouble finding places at other temples. He felt lucky to have been accepted at Chingyeh. His friend had been turned down. The problem, he said, was that tourism had turned Shaolin into a retirement home, and anyone who stayed there was assumed to be more interested in comfort and fame than the Dharma.

We worked our way through the fog, back over the ridge, across the bridge, and out onto the road again. An hour later, we passed another sandbar of houses. This was Ertaochiao. *Ch'iao* means "bridge," but there was no trace of one.

When Steve and I came here in August, we waded across the river. Past a couple of farmhouses on the other side, at the mouth of a side valley, we found the hut of Ch'uan-fu.

She was thirty-seven. At seventeen, she had become a Taoist nun. Three years later, she switched to Buddhism and spent five years at Fengte and Tsaotang temples. Afterward, she tried to live on Kuanyinshan but had nearly starved to death. She had been living in the hut where we met her for the past three years. She said she was able to buy what she needed with money she made from collecting herbs. I don't think anyone except the local farmers had ever visited her before. Talking about her life and practice, she came close to tears. She was lonely. And her roof leaked. She said, "You can't live in the mountains if you're still attached, if you haven't seen through the red dust. Life in the mountains is hard. But once you've seen through the illusions of this world, hardships aren't important. The only thing that matters is practice. If you don't practice, you'll never get free of the dust of delusion."

When I asked if Steve could take her picture, she went inside and came back out wearing her formal robes that she kept for special occasions. Afterward, we said good-bye, and Steve and I worked our way farther into the valley. The trail skirted the slope, then criss-crossed the stream. After less than an hour, we heard the sound of mallets, and soon we reached a small clearing that was half filled by a large hut.

This was the home of Ch'e-hui. It was in good condition, and unlike Ch'uan-fu's thatched hut, it had a tiled roof. Several farmers were pounding the green rinds off walnuts. Ch'e-hui was standing outside. As soon as she saw us coming, she went inside and brought out stools. We exchanged greetings and sat down. Two other women came out. One was Ch'e-hui's sister. The other was her disciple. While her disciple went to haul water and make tea, Ch'e-hui told us that she was from Chilin Province and that she had come to this area with her family in the 1950s. They had come to work on the highway being built between Tienshui and Lanchou to the west and ended up staying. In 1957, she announced that she wanted to become a nun. Her parents and brothers had disapproved, but she refused to change her mind. After studying Buddhism for five years in a temple, she came up the Feng River gorge and built a hut next to West Kuanyin Temple. Seven years later, she moved again and built her present hut, where she had been living for the last twenty years. She was seventy-four. I guess Ch'uan-fu was still on my mind. I asked her if she ever got lonely.

Ch'e-hui: No, I like living alone. I can't leave this mountain. Every time I leave, I want to come back right away. Also, I have a disciple, so I don't get lonely.

Q: How often do you go down the mountain?

Ch'uan-fu in formal robes in front of her hut.

Ch'e-hui: I go down to the village about once a month to buy things like flour and salt, cooking oil and kerosene. If I don't need anything, I don't go down. I plant all the vegetables I need, and the potatoes last all winter. During the summer, I work every day in the garden. Usually there's something to eat. When there's not, I don't worry about it.

Q: Do you get much help from other monks and nuns in the area?

Ch'e-hui: No, we depend on ourselves. If I need money, my family tries to help me. My sister is visiting me right now. It's the first time we've seen each other in almost thirty years. After working thirty-six years for a trading unit in Shenyang, she finally retired earlier this year. She's sick now and wanted to see me before she died. She's been here a month now. We don't need much. We don't spend more than 10 to 20 RMB a month [two to four dollars]. We're very frugal. For example, we only use about one kilo of cooking oil a month. Also, I have four walnut trees. Some years I can get more than 100 RMB for my walnuts. For the past two days, these farmers have been helping me harvest them.

Q: Do you practice very much?

Ch'e-hui: Every night before I go to bed I meditate. And every morning and evening I chant the *Titsang Sutra* and the *Diamond Sutra.* I only attended the first grade, but I've learned to read the characters in the sutras. I can tell you from my own experience that you can achieve something if you practice. If you don't practice, you achieve nothing.

Q: Were you affected by the Cultural Revolution?

Ch'e-hui: Not much. They came and took away my incense and my incense burner. But I hid my Buddha statue. They didn't arrest me, and they never came back again. I kept practicing the same as before. But other monks and nuns had a lot of trouble, especially those who lived in temples. Many were forced to leave their temples and return to the world of red dust. One monk who was forced to return to his family owned this mountain. He didn't have anything else and wanted to sell it to me. My family finally managed to collect 300 RMB [sixty dollars], and he signed the deed over to me. When the Red Guards came, they took the deed. They couldn't read and thought it was religious propaganda. When I tried to get it back, they said I was a counterrevolutionary, and they burned it. I've been trying to get the government to give me a new deed, but they don't pay any attention to an old nun like me.

Q: Do people ever come up here to visit you?

Ch'e-hui: No, no one. Especially not foreigners.

A fine mist was beginning to fall, and we said good-bye. On our way back, as we approached the river, Ch'uan-fu met us with a huge sack of walnuts. It must have weighed twenty kilos. I'd given her enough money to fix her roof, and she insisted we accept the walnuts. She said it was all she had. We thanked her and somehow managed to get the walnuts across the river and back to Sian.

That was in August, when the river was easy to ford. Now it was late March, and an all-night rain had turned the river dark and dangerous, full of tree limbs. This time, I walked past Ertaochiao, and thirty minutes later I was back at Chingyeh Temple. I thanked the young monk for serving as my guide. I think he was finally as tired as I was, and he disappeared into his room. Back in my room, I poured most of a thermos of hot water into a basin and took a bath, using my bandana as washrag and towel. After changing into clean clothes, I used the rest of the water in the thermos to make a cup of instant coffee. I ate the last of the homemade cookies my friend Mountain Dave had given me in Taiwan; then I fell asleep. I slept through dinner and didn't wake up until the next morning.

After another breakfast of cornmeal porridge, K'ai-lung asked me if there was anywhere else I'd like to visit. I'd already been to Tao-hsuan's pagoda on the peak as well as to Pai Chu-yi's nearby grave. (As one of the T'ang dynasty's greatest poets, Pai Chu-yi had a certain responsibility to the public and had a second, more accessible, grave in Loyang.) I suggested a visit to Wofo Temple on Chinghuashan to the east, and K'ai-lung agreed to show me the way.

A munitions plant blocked access to Chinghuashan from the road, so K'ai-lung led the way to a less conspicuous approach along an adjoining ridge. The trail, in fact, was a ridge run, and it took us only about ninety minutes to hike the three kilometers that separated the two temples. Just after reaching the summit, we heard the sound of cannon fire far below.

The temple was a hodgepodge of small buildings clustered around a rocky peak. One of the buildings enclosed a cliff from which a reclining buddha had been carved less than two hundred years earlier by a former abbot of Chingyeh Temple. Inside another building, we met four laymen and one laywoman who were there not to practice but to cater to the occasional pilgrims and weekend tourists. We joined our hosts in bowls of noodles, and K'ai-lung broached the subject of Chingyeh Temple reassuming control of Wofo Temple. The first thing he wanted to do, he said, was to get rid of all the buildings that cluttered the peak. The only response was the slurping of noodles. As soon as we finished eating, we said good-bye and headed back.

It was only the second time that K'ai-lung had been to Chinghuashan, and we got lost in the fog. Fortunately, the ridge was hard to miss, and we soon found the trail again. Although he was only twenty-five, K'ai-lung had a good understanding of the practical problems involved in reestablishing the temples in the area as places of practice. His long-range plan, and I assumed it was also that of Master Miao in Hsiamen, who was financing much of the operation, was to link Fengte and Wofo temples with Chingyeh into a major center of practice, to discourage tourism, and to refuse any assistance from the government, including electricity. K'ai-lung said that once the temple accepted such assistance, the government would begin demanding that certain things be done or not be done. The government, according to all the monks and nuns I talked to, was not interested in supporting religious practice, only tourism.

About ten minutes before the final bend that brought Chingyeh Temple into view, K'ai-lung suggested we visit an area known as Tung-

kou, or East Gully. This was where Tao-hsuan's disciples and their successors had built a series of huts, forty-eight of them, that were handed
down from one hermit to another, until they were destroyed or abandoned during the Cultural Revolution. K'ai-lung said the huts were
now being rebuilt.

A trail down the south slope of the ridge soon led us to the first hut.
Set just above the stream that ran through the gully, it was surrounded
by several small patches of land that had been cleared for vegetables.
Construction of the hut had been completed the day before. It was
made of adobe, and the bricks, I learned, weren't sun-dried but laid
in place as soon as they were formed. The bricks were still wet, and
the two monks who were planning to move in had fired up the ovens
that were built into the hut's two adobe beds to dry the place out. The
roof was tiled, and the windows had frames that looked as if they
would someday see some glass. One of the two Peking University
graduates planning to live there said it took six workmen two weeks
to build and cost 500 RMB, a hundred bucks. It looked like it would
last a lifetime.

Chapter Seven

Cloud
People

*U*ntil it was eclipsed by such cities as Loyang, Kaifeng, Hangchou, and Peking, Ch'ang-an was the center of China, the capital of eleven dynasties, the hub of an empire that stretched from Korea to Vietnam and from the Pacific to Persia. During its peak in the seventh and eighth centuries, Ch'ang-an was the biggest and most populated city in the ancient world. It was the sea into which all cultural and economic streams in China flowed, and its greatest marketplace. Situated at the eastern end of the Silk Road, it was also China's first cosmopolitan city. As soon as it was built in 200 B.C., Ch'ang-an became a city of travelers.

My most lasting impression of Ch'ang-an's modern incarnation as Sian is of thousands of people walking around wearing white caps, floating and swirling through the streets like so many clouds. A substantial percentage of the city's population is of Central Asiatic origin, and the white caps are another version of the head covering common in all Islamic cultures. There are also large communities of Manchurians, Mongolians, and Tibetans. A tourist pamphlet lists thirty-eight minorities. In 1990, the city's population was three million. Sixty years ago, it was less than two hundred thousand.

It's still a city of travelers, and its symbol, appropriately, is a wild goose, the legacy of Hsuan-tsang, the city's most famous traveler. Hsuan-tsang left Ch'ang-an in 629 for India to resolve his doubts concerning the Buddha's teaching that this world is nothing but mind. When he reached India two years later, he began to study the Mind-Only doctrine with the last great teachers of the Yogacara lineage. Fifteen years later, in 645, Emperor T'ai-tsung welcomed him back to Ch'ang-an with the pomp usually reserved for victorious generals.

T'ai-tsung wanted to know everything that Hsuan-tsang had seen and heard on his journey, and the monk had no choice but to satisfy the emperor's curiosity. The result was Hsuan-tsang's *Record of Western Regions* and a unique friendship. As time went on, Hsuan-tsang's account was transmogrified into *Journey to the West,* one of China's best-known and best-loved stories. Hsuan-tsang, however, wasn't interested in writing stories or travel gazetteers. He was anxious to begin translating the sutras he had brought back from India. In 648, the crown prince invited him to set up a translation center in the capital at Tzuen Temple, which he had constructed as a memorial to his mother.

Not long after Hsuan-tsang moved in, he became concerned that a fire or storm might destroy the priceless scriptures he had taken so long to collect. He asked T'ai-tsung for permission to build a pagoda to store them in, and the emperor agreed. The women of the palace donated their jewels to pay for its construction, and it was completed in 652.

Soon after it was built, successful candidates of the imperial exams started signing their names near the archways that looked out in the four directions from the upper storeys. The lists of names reminded people of columns of migrating geese, and they started calling the structure Tayenta, Big Goose Pagoda. At the end of a poem commemorating his own group signing in 752, Tu Fu wrote:

> *the gosling leaves on its journey*
> *crying where will it rest*
> *look at the wild geese following the sun*
> *each of them searching for grain*

The name stuck, and it's been called Big Goose Pagoda ever since. And it's still at the southeast corner of the city—all sixty-four meters. But the columns of wild geese are gone. The only names I could find dated back no earlier than two hundred years ago: Ch'ing dynasty graffiti. Outside, I stopped to read the prefaces to Hsuan-tsang's translations on two steles on either side of the entrance. They were composed by Emperor T'ai-tsung and the crown prince and written by Chu Sui-liang, one of China's greatest calligraphers. For several years they had served as models for my own efforts at calligraphy. It was like meeting an old teacher.

During the T'ang dynasty, the temple was also famous for its peonies, which bloom in April and May. A few dozen bushes lined the path below the main shrine hall, and a monk told me they still attracted crowds during their weeks of glory. The temple grounds, though, had been reduced to one-tenth their former size, and the thirty monks living there seemed but caretakers of a memory. When one of them told me Hsuan-tsang's remains were at another temple near the Chungnan Mountains, I hired a car and driver and headed for the mountains.

We drove southeast on the road that began at the north end of the temple. One kilometer later, we passed through a village that bore the name of the city's most famous ancient resort, the Chuchiang Waterway.

It had begun simply enough during the Ch'in and Han dynasties with a pond fed by a natural spring and around which trees and flowers were planted. During subsequent dynasties, the pond was expanded on a huge scale, and during the seventh and eighth centuries it became a zigzagging course of waterfalls, streams, and ponds that covered an area two kilometers from east to west and four kilometers from north to south. A canal was constructed all the way from the Chungnan Mountains to keep it supplied with water. Pavilions and villas lined its banks. In spring, the imperial court gathered here to view the apricot blossoms on the west bank. In summer, they came to view the lotuses along the east bank.

It was also here that a drinking game originated that relied on the vagaries of water and wind. The game started with a jug of wine placed on a wooden vessel and allowed to drift along the waterway until it reached one of the participants, who would pour himself a cup of wine, dash off a line of poetry on a scroll provided, then shove the vessel back out. The game ended when everyone was too drunk to write or there was no more wine. It ended permanently when there was no more water. Travelers who visited Ch'ang-an in the tenth century say that the pavilions were in ruins and the waterway was planted with corn. But memories linger, and people still call this one of the province's eight wonders.

Just past the village, we turned onto a dirt road that ended a minute later at a place called Hanyao, a gully that wound several hundred meters into the loess plateau. This was where Wang Pao-ch'uan waited eighteen years for her husband.

Wang Pao-ch'uan was the youngest daughter of a T'ang dynasty prime minister anxious to arrange a politically useful marriage. When she refused to marry any of the men suggested by her father, she was forced to climb Big Goose Pagoda, toss down a silk ball, and marry whoever caught it. When she saw a poor traveler she had met the night before, she threw the ball to him and he caught it. His name was Hsueh P'ing-kuei. Pao-ch'uan's father, however, refused to acknowledge Hsueh and sent him away. And when Pao-ch'uan refused to accept her father's decision, she was ordered to leave as well. The young couple had no place to live, so they moved into a former kiln that had been carved into the loess walls of Hanyao.

Not long afterward, war broke out with the nomadic Tanguts to the north, and P'ing-kuei offered his services. Unfortunately, the army was under the command of one of the prime minister's sons-in-law, who set a trap for P'ing-kuei that resulted in his capture by the enemy.

Despite reports of her husband's death, Pao-ch'uan continued to wait faithfully for his return at Hanyao. Eighteen years later, peace was restored with the Tanguts, and P'ing-kuei was released. When he returned to Ch'ang-an, he found his wife outside their cave picking a wild vegetable called *chi-ts'ai*, or shepherd's purse. She had been living on it all the years he was gone.

After visiting her cave, we stopped at a food stall at the entrance to the gully and ate an early lunch of boiled *chiao-tzu*, or dumplings. They were filled with freshly picked shepherd's purse. The flavor was slightly pungent, and I imagined Wang Pao-ch'uan at least hadn't found it dull.

We returned to the main road and headed southeast again, but not for long. A minute later, we turned right onto a dirt road that led through fields of millet and corn, past two brick kilns, and up the dirt slope of Fenghsi Plateau to Hu-hai's small, bramble-covered grave mound.

Hu-hai was the son of the Ch'in dynasty's First Emperor, who died in 210 B.C. Hu-hai reigned as Second Emperor for three years, all of them at the pleasure of the eunuch Chao Kao. Chao once brought a deer before the young emperor and said it was a horse. No one dared contradict the eunuch, and the emperor thought he was hallucinating. Two weeks later, Chao arranged another "hallucination" by ordering soldiers dressed as bandits to "attack" the palace. The emperor promptly committed suicide and was replaced with another puppet.

Though grave robbers have doubtlessly done their work, Hu-hai's mound hasn't been excavated, and it's seldom visited by tourists. It's located at the south end of the basin that was once the Chuchiang Waterway. I could still make out the promontory below the grave mound where emperors entertained successful exam candidates at Purple Cloud Pavilion. After the banquet, they would stroll along the shoreline to Big Goose Pagoda, sign their names, and turn into geese.

Back on the main road, we continued south along the ancient course of the Huangchu Canal. It once supplied the waterway and presumably will do so again. One of the caretakers at Hu-hai's grave told me that the government had drawn up plans to restore the waterway and create a large park. He said a dam had already been built for the purpose at the mouth of Tayu Gorge in the Chungnan Mountains.

We stopped again four kilometers past Hu-hai's grave, just before the village of Tungwu. To our left on Tuling Plateau was a series of grave mounds. One of them was less than two hundred meters from the road, and we walked through fields of ankle-high millet sprouts to inspect the site. It included one central mound flanked by two smaller mounds and a "spirit-way" of twelve stone statues of horses and officials to welcome visitors. They were all carved from single blocks of granite and all in remarkably good condition. Equally remarkable was that the site had been left in the care of local villagers. I picked up a roof tile and showed it to a farmer. He said historians had visited the site but had been unable to determine whose grave it was. An old map I found later listed it as the grave of Hsien-ti, the last emperor of the Han dynasty, who died in A.D. 220.

A short walk east of Hsien-ti's grave was a much bigger mound that rose at least a hundred meters above the plateau. The farmer and the old map agreed that it was the grave of Emperor Hsuan-ti, who died in 49 B.C. I scanned the surrounding plateau with binoculars. There were grave mounds everywhere.

We walked back to the car and drove southeast for fifteen kilometers to the market town of Yinchen. From here, both the road and the route of the old Huangchu Canal extended south another six kilometers to the new dam at the mouth of Tayu Gorge. Past Tayu Gorge was Chiawutai, a mountain famous among Buddhists since the T'ang dynasty for its precipitous summit and the seclusion it afforded. I had already visited Chiawutai twice with Steve, and I planned to climb it again.

But first, I wanted to stop at Hsingchiao Temple eight kilometers east of Yinchen. A few minutes later, we reached the temple's long red walls at the western edge of Shaoling Plateau. Rising behind the wall, like the trunk of a giant cedar, Hsuan-tsang's twenty-three-meter pagoda dominated the temple. After his death in 664, his relics were placed in a pagoda near the capital on White Deer Plateau. But the constant sight of Hsuan-tsang's pagoda so saddened the emperor, it was moved here in 669. And here it has stood ever since, twenty kilometers south of the capital and within view of the Chungnan Mountains that Hsuan-tsang once described as the "grandfather of all mountains."

Hsuan-tsang's pagoda was much smaller than its model, Big Goose Pagoda, but it towered above two adjacent three-storey pagodas containing the relics of Hsuan-tsang's most famous disciples, K'uei-chi and Yuan-tse. Over the centuries, the pagodas of these three founders of the Mind-Only school of Chinese Buddhism had successfully weathered wars and natural disasters. The shrine halls hadn't been so fortunate. They were destroyed and rebuilt several times, most recently in 1939 by Chiang Kai-shek in memory of his mother. The main structures were still in fairly good condition, thanks to Chou En-lai, who had ordered the temple protected even during the Cultural Revolution.

Over the entrance to the main shrine hall hung a plaque bearing the words "Hsingchiao Temple," written by the poet-philosopher K'ang Yu-wei. In 1898 Emperor Kuang-hsu appointed K'ang to reform the empire upon modern lines, but the attempt was derailed by Empress Dowager Tzu-hsi and her clique, and K'ang had to flee to Japan. Although he eventually returned, K'ang ended his life in seclusion, all but ignored by the founders of the Republic. His calligraphy on the plaque was dated 1923, four years before his death at the age of sixty-nine.

The main shrine hall wasn't especially memorable, but the rear hall contained some impressive treasures. Besides several Ming dynasty paintings of Buddhist deities, there were three bronze statues of Kuan-yin, Bodhisattva of Compassion, dating back to the T'ang dynasty. During his travels, whenever Hsuan-tsang was in trouble, it was Kuan-yin's name he invoked. I lit some incense and asked the attendant if I could talk with the abbot.

After a few minutes, the attendant returned and led me into the abbot's bedroom, which also served as his office. He was sitting behind a large desk. The top consisted of a huge slab of yellow onyx—a gift to the temple from Chiang Kai-shek. The abbot's name was Ch'ang-ming. I introduced myself and explained that I was visiting hermits in the area.

During the course of our conversation, Ch'ang-ming said he was seventy-four and from Hsienyang, just west of Sian. After becoming a monk in 1937, he moved to the Chungnan Mountains and lived at Tzuchulin, or Purple Bamboo Hermitage, on Nanwutai. He stayed there for nearly twenty years with his master, Fo-ch'en, until the authorities began chasing monks out of the mountains. In 1956, he traveled to Peking to study at the capital's Buddhist academy and returned two years later to rejoin Fo-ch'en, who had been appointed abbot of Hsingchiao Temple. When Fo-ch'en died in 1981, Ch'ang-ming took over as abbot; he was also deputy director of the Shensi Buddhist Association. I asked him why he chose the Chungnan Mountains when he started to practice.

Ch'ang-ming: People have been coming to the Chungnan Mountains to practice ever since Buddhism came to China. Even monks and nuns from south China come here to practice. They stay for three to five years, then return to the south to set up their own practice centers. This is where monks and nuns come who leave home for the Dharma. Practice isn't something that you can do in a few days. It takes years before you really begin to achieve anything. It isn't easy. But people who come here to practice aren't afraid of hardship. That's why they come here. Many of them have become enlightened in these mountains, and many of them have gone on to become great teachers. In modern times, Hsu-yun and Yin-fa lived on Chiawutai; Yin-kuang and Lai-kuo lived on Nanwutai. This is where they achieved enlightenment. Everyone knows these mountains are a good place to practice. That's why I chose them.

Ch'ang-ming wasn't very talkative, although he was helpful. He showed me the sutra library that occupied the temple's east wing. It contained a number of important reprints of the *Tripitaka,* or Buddhist Canon, but none of Hsuan-tsang's original manuscripts. Afterward, in the monastery store, I bought a rubbing of Hsuan-tsang wearing his ingenious sutra backpack. It was from a temple stele carved in 1933.

Ch'ang-ming said that although both he and Fo-ch'en had lived on Nanwutai, fifteen kilometers to the southwest, Hsingchiao Temple had a special relationship with Chiawutai, which was less than ten kilometers to the south. He said that hermits from Chiawutai came to Hsingchiao Temple when they got too sick or too old to support themselves anymore, and young monks from Hsingchiao Temple still went to Chiawutai to deepen their practice.

Ch'ang-ming told me to wait outside the shrine hall. A few minutes later, he returned with an old monk whom he introduced as Kuangshan. He said Kuang-shan had lived for more than forty years on the back side of Chiawutai in a hut not far above the one Hsu-yun occupied at the turn of the last century. Kuang-shan was ninety-eight years old. He had come down the mountain the year before when he could no longer work the slopes. I asked Kuang-shan if there were any other hermits still living on Chiawutai. I could barely hear his answers, and Ch'ang-ming had to repeat what he said.

Kuang-shan: Yes, a few, but not as many as before.

Q: Where did you live?

Kuang-shan: At Fohui Maopeng, just above Shihtzu Maopeng. [The word *maopeng* means "hut," though its usage is sometimes extended to include a small temple or hermitage.]

Q: What about Shihtzu Maopeng, Hsu-yun's former hut? Is there anyone living there?

Kuang-shan: Several monks have stayed there since Hsu-yun left. But I'm not sure if anyone is there now. The trail isn't easy. A college student came up a while back and planned to move in, but I don't know if he ever did.

Ch'ang-ming: Two monks moved up to Hsu-yun's hut about a month ago, but I'm not sure how long they plan to stay.

Q: If it's so hard to reach, why did you live there?

Kuang-shan: For the quiet. Zen monks like quiet.

Q: Have conditions changed much on Chiawutai?

Kuang-shan: It's still quiet. Monks and nuns still go up there to practice. A few small temples and huts have been repaired. People still practice. A few monks and nuns live in the foothills too.

Q: When you lived there, what sutras did you read?

Kuang-shan: I didn't read sutras. I just chanted the name of the Buddha, Amita Buddha. And I meditated. I practiced Zen. Zen monks don't read sutras.

Q: How did you get enough to eat?

Kuang-shan: Everyone who lives in the mountains plants a few vegetables and gathers wild plants. I planted everything I needed. I didn't come down unless there was a good reason. I had enough food.

Q: How often did you come down?

Kuang-shan: No telling. Sometimes once every couple of years. Now I'm too weak to live there anymore.

Kuang-shan was exhausted, and Ch'ang-ming helped him back inside.

I had visited Chiawutai twice already with Steve. On both occasions, the route we had taken was south from Yinchen to the village of Tayu, up a hill to the dam that now blocked the mouth of Tayu Gorge, by ferry to the end of the reservoir, and then along a rocky road to a stone bridge next to the remains of Wuli Temple. A trail on the other side of the river led up a side gorge and eventually Chiawutai's east slope. This time, I wanted to climb the west slope. When Ch'ang-ming came back outside, he agreed to show me the way.

We drove back to the main road and zigzagged our way across the countryside. Twice, Ch'ang-ming had to ask directions from farmers. After about twenty minutes, we started up the base of the Chungnan Mountains. When the gradient became too steep for the car, we stopped.

The traditional route up Chiawutai's west slope was via Paitao Gorge, and the gorge was less than one kilometer away. Looking back,

Ch'ang-ming pointed out the former site of Hsin-an Temple at the south end of the village we had just passed. He said it had been one of the most important temples in the Chungnan Mountains and had housed several hundred monks as late as 1949. Now it was the village school. Ch'ang-ming turned toward the mountains and said the road continued up the gorge for several more kilometers and then became a trail of stone steps. There were several hermits living up side gorges, he said, but they would be hard to find and I wouldn't have enough time if I planned to reach Chiawutai by sunset, which he estimated was three hours away.

While the driver turned the car around, Ch'ang-ming wrote something on a slip of paper. He said I might want to include a poem by a fellow hermit among the materials I was collecting. It was by Ch'ang-hui, another disciple of Fo-ch'en. After we said good-bye, and Ch'ang-ming disappeared down the road, I read Ch'ang-hui's poem:

> *on a peak standing still*
> *only clouds coming and going*
> *a thousand misty mountains below me*
>
> *in the open sitting straight*
> *nothing false nothing real*
> *shapes of light and dark before me*

It was early April, and there were still patches of snow on the north slope. I followed the road into Paitao Gorge and after about two kilometers reached a pile of stones masquerading as Taipai Temple. It was named for the eighth-century poet Li Pai, whose sobriquet was T'ai-pai. Inside, I met Ch'ang-hua, a sixty-six-year-old Buddhist nun from Lanchou. She said she had been a nun for more than forty years and had been living at Taipai Temple for the last ten. She said the temple was in ruins when she first arrived, then added that good places weren't good for practice. The walls now had a roof, but the place was still in ruins. She told me she had been wearing the same set of clothes for five years, but she was generous with her tea and sugar. After quenching my thirst and lighting some incense for Li Pai, I said good-bye and continued on my way.

After one more kilometer, I passed another small temple at a place called Second Gate to Heaven. There was a new shrine hall and a new adobe hut, but no one was at home, so I kept going. Just past the temple, the road ended at a place called Cold Spring, and I began climbing a long flight of stone steps. Thirty minutes later, I caught up to a monk who was carrying a twenty-five-kilo sack of flour on his shoulders. We both took a break. He said his name was Yu-yuan. He was forty-three, from Sian, and he turned out to be the new occupant of Shihtzu Maopeng, Hsu-yun's former hut on the back side of Chiawutai. I asked him how long it took him to go through a sack of flour. He said a twenty-five-kilo bag usually lasted two monks about forty days.

I said I'd heard that two monks were living on the back side of Chiawutai. He said the other monk was Yin-hui, from Paochi, also forty-three, and the occupant of a new hut a few hundred meters below Shihtzu Maopeng. Yu-yuan said that he and Yin-hui had spent several years looking for a suitable place to practice before finally deciding on the back side of Chiawutai. He said they had already brought up bedding and a few other necessities and were now stockpiling provisions so they wouldn't have to go down so often. They planned to stay as long as it took. We talked for a few minutes about practice, then agreed we'd better be moving on.

Twenty minutes later, I reached a flat-topped ridge known as Fenshuiling. A small Taoist shrine to Kuan-ti, the God of War, was locked. Looking down from the west side of the ridge, I could see Yu-yuan struggling up the steps with the flour that he and Yin-hui would eventually turn into steamed buns, fried bread, and noodles. Looking down the east side of the ridge, I could see the trail that Steve and I had taken the previous September.

In September, we didn't follow the trail to Fenshuiling. Just before the path crossed the stream for the last time, we turned left and headed for a farmhouse about a hundred meters farther up the gorge. The farmer was home and agreed to guide us to Hsu-yun's Shihtzu

Maopeng, or Lion Hut, on the back side of Chiawutai. The trail began just beyond his house and led up a long valley.

After about thirty minutes, we heard a jingling sound. A few seconds later, a monk appeared out of the jungle of growth that covered the trail. The jingling was coming from his wooden staff. It had iron rings on the top to ward off evil spirits and to warn wild animals to clear the path. The bottom end was fitted with a small iron spade for use in negotiating slippery slopes. He said his name was Kuo-shan and that he was from Shanyang County, about a hundred kilometers to the southeast. He was sixty-seven years old, and he had lived at Tayi Cave for the last ten of them. I asked him about the hardships of living on the mountain.

Kuo-shan: It's all the same to me. It just looks hard to you.

Q: What sutras do you study?

Kuo-shan: I can't read. I never went to school. I just meditate.

Q: Why do you live so far away from people?

Kuo-shan: I'm a monk. I've seen through the world of red dust. As long as I have enough to eat, I stay on the mountain. I live by myself. When I run out of food, I go down. That's why I'm going to the village today. I'm out of provisions.

Q: Are there any other people living in huts on this side?

Kuo-shan: Besides me, there's one other monk.

Q: Where does he live?

Kuo-shan: Right up there above that cliff. [He pointed to a cave just south of the summit.]

Q: How much farther is it to Lion Hut?

Kuo-shan: It's another two hours up this trail just over the ridge. Why don't you stay for a few days? I should be back with provisions later this afternoon.

Kuo-shan coming down the Chiawutai trail.

I told him our driver was waiting for us to return to the dam. Perhaps next time. We said good-bye and hiked up a slope covered with yellow wildflowers and dense foliage. The trail was hardly visible, and we often lost sight of one another. Our guide periodically disappeared into the bushes and reappeared with different kinds of wild fruit: Chinese gooseberries bigger than any Kiwi fruit I'd ever seen and something resembling a pomegranate or passion fruit with sweet, milky seeds.

It was early fall, and we must have brushed against some sort of poisonous plant. When Steve and I returned to Taiwan, strings of blisters appeared on our hands and arms and legs. Calamine and other lotions had no effect. A Chinese doctor finally gave me some salve and herbal pills, and the blisters vanished. During my next visit to the mountains, I learned we had contracted mild cases of lacquer poisoning. The lacquer tree is a variety of sumac native to the Chungnan Mountains. It's the source of the resin used in making lacquer ware and is highly poisonous. People overly sensitive to it can turn into human balloons. In a village along the Feng River gorge, Steve and I once saw a boy whose face was so swollen from lacquer poisoning that he couldn't see.

As we worked our way up the mountain, we passed the remains of five or six huts. There were probably more, but the vines and tall grass made it difficult to see anything that wasn't carved into the cliffs. Obviously, this was once a popular mountain with hermits.

After hiking for more than an hour, we finally reached the ridge and started down the other side. Ten minutes later, we passed Fohui Hut, where Kuang-shan had lived until he had become too weak to support himself. His old garden was lost beneath the weeds.

After a few more minutes, we reached Hsu-yun's Lion Hut. It was built of piled stones against a huge boulder that faced south. According to the farmer, the tiled roof was added by another hermit about twenty years ago. There was room for a small garden in front, but judging from the weeds, no one had lived there for some time.

Hsu-yun spent three years here at the beginning of the century. In

1900, the Boxer Rebellion and the arrival of foreign troops forced the imperial court to flee Peking, and Emperor Kuang-hsu and Empress Dowager Tzu-hsi set up a temporary capital in Sian. Hsu-yun arrived in Sian about the same time. In his *Hsuyun Hoshang Nienpu*, he recorded the following notes for the years 1900 to 1903, when he was in his sixties:

> In the tenth month, I left the city in secret and entered the Chung-nan Mountains to build a hut. On the back side of Chiawutai, I found a suitably secluded place called Lion Cliff. To avoid unnecessary visi-tors, I changed my name to Hsu-yun [Empty Cloud]. There wasn't enough water on the mountain, and I had to melt snow. To satisfy my hunger, I ate wild plants. . . .
>
> On the winter solstice of the following year, I went to Sian to buy some things for Ch'ing-shan, who was the most respected monk on the mountain and with whom I had developed a close relationship. On the way back, I got caught in a snowstorm. Halfway up the mountain, I slipped and fell down a crevice. Fortunately, I landed in a snow bank. Another hermit heard me yelling and came to my rescue. My clothes were soaked, and it was almost nightfall. But I had to keep going. I knew that the trail would be impassable by morning. Long after dark, I reached Ch'ing-shan's hut. When he saw my sorry state, he laughed and said I was a hopeless case. I returned to my hut and stayed there for the rest of the spring and summer. . . .
>
> By the end of the year, the mountains were covered with snow again, and the cold was intense. But even though I lived alone in a poor hut, my mind was completely unaffected. One day, after putting a pot of potatoes on the fire to cook, I sat cross-legged waiting until they were done. Suddenly, I entered *samadhi* [Sanskrit for an undistracted mind].
>
> Fu-ch'eng and several other monks living nearby were puzzled that I hadn't called on them for some time and decided to pay me a visit to exchange new year's greetings. Outside my hut, they saw tiger tracks in the snow but no human footprints. When they opened my door, they saw I had entered *samadhi*. One of them struck a stone chime. As I returned to consciousness, they asked me if I had eaten. I said, "Not yet, but the potatoes must be done by now." As I lifted the cover of the cauldron, I found the potatoes covered with an inch of mold.

Empty Cloud's former hut.

Several days later, Empty Cloud left for a more remote section of the Chungnan Mountains "to avoid the trouble of meeting people." He spent the rest of his long life wandering from temple to temple and helping restore a number of them. When he died in 1959 at Yunchushan in Kiangsi Province at the age of one hundred and twenty, he was the most respected monk in China. He still is.

Eight months after Empty Cloud left Chiawutai, the mountain was visited by the Buddhist layman Kao Ho-nien, who left this account in his *Mingshan Yufangchi:*

> On the twelfth day of the eighth month of 1903, I left Ch'ang-an, and after eighty *li* [two *li* equal one kilometer] I passed through the villages of Wangmang and Liuhsiu and arrived at Paitao Gorge, where the Chungnan Mountains begin. I started climbing and after fifteen *li* reached Hukuo Temple at Poshan Rock. People call this Chiawutai. I stayed in Pen-ch'ang's hut, which he called Little Stairway and which was where Tz'u-pen formerly stayed. The mountain was majestic and beyond the sound of dogs or roosters or the sight of the dusty world. Living here alone in a hut, a person could easily forget the humdrum world.
>
> On Midautumn Festival (the fifteenth, or full moon, of the eighth month), I invited forty or fifty hermits living on the mountain to a special ceremony and a vegetarian feast. Later, as I returned to my hut, I stopped outside the door and gazed at the mountains in the moonlight. The moon looked lovely and the world at peace. In the valley behind the mountain, I arranged to have two huts built for Tz'u-fa and Chueh-k'u. Also, I invited all the monks on the mountain to Hukuo Temple for forty-nine days of concentrated meditation. I made arrangements for food and fuel and provided new padded robes and blankets for the ten senior monks who stayed through the new year . . .
>
> On New Year's Day, I climbed to the back side of the summit along a dangerous dragon spine that dropped off on both sides. I visited Wu-hua Cave, where Tsung-mi, the Fifth Patriarch of the Huayen school, discovered the Way. The cave was occupied by Te-an. [Hsu-yun says Tao-ming lived here.] I asked him if he was at peace [a pun on his name, which means the peace of virtue]. He said that living beyond the world and spending his time in meditation, how could he have any

worries? Two *li* farther on, I came to Kuanyin Cave. It was occupied by a monk from Kiangsi intent on being reborn in the Western Paradise.

I continued another five *li* to Chinghuashan [apparently a mistake; he must have meant Hsuehhuashan]. Its strange rock formations jutted through the clouds, and its trees were covered with snow. The trail was steep, but there was a hut at the top. I climbed up, but whoever lived there was gone. [Kao must be referring to the nun T'ien-jan who died in 1919 after living at the summit of Hsuehhuashan for fifty years.] Afterward, I went down the mountain to Weimo Hut. Chueh-k'u and Ts'u-fa greeted me, and we talked late into the night about living in the mountains and forgetting about the mountains.

The next morning, I continued down to Tayi Cave, where Ta-fang was practicing austerities. Ting-hui agreed to accompany me down the back side of the mountain. For the next five *li* the trail was precipitous, and the ice was slippery. The other monks advised us not to go. But I said people trying to reach paradise don't stop just because the road is hard. We crossed the ridge and started down the other side. The weather changed, and it looked like it was about to snow. The trail felt like oil, but we managed to reach Hsiu-yuan's hut. He had lived there for more than ten years. I asked him if he ever got lonely. He said, "No, not as long as I have the wind and the moon, the water and the mountains for my companions."

I also visited Fu-ch'eng's hut, and he accompanied me to Tao-ming's hut. Tao-ming had lived on the back side for twenty years. I asked him if anyone else lived in the mountains beyond his hut. He said, "People have reported seeing an old monk with hair below his knees who looks several hundred years old. I've never seen him, but sometimes I hear the sound of chanting. I can't tell where it's coming from, though."

I asked him what sort of food there was in the mountains. He said, "This mountain isn't as good as others around here, and sometimes I have to go down in late summer to beg for leftover grain. But usually I have enough by planting a few potatoes and gathering wild plants. There's enough firewood, but there isn't much water. Sometimes in summer I have to carry water up from far below. This ridge is high, and the cold is intense. Not much grows here, and not many people come this far. The path is hard and dangerous. Only someone in good health whose mind is set on the Way can survive here."

It was getting late, and Steve and I decided not to venture any farther than Empty Cloud's hut. After Steve took a few pictures, our guide told us there was still enough time to reach the mountain's summit, but we would have to hurry. We returned to the ridge, then set off on a path that only our guide could see. In some places we had to pull ourselves up by vines. Finally, after about an hour, we reached the southern end of the summit's long spine. After letting us catch our breath, our guide led us off on a side trail to Kuanyin Cave, an incredible retreat built into the east cliff. It included a small, grassy ledge and a cistern carved out of the cliff for storing rainwater. I tried to imagine sitting there on a moonlit night. I imagined floating in space.

A few minutes later, at the northern end of the summit, we knocked on the back gate of Hsingching Temple. After a long wait, the abbot opened the gate, then quickly disappeared into the kitchen. We must have looked as exhausted as we felt. He reappeared a few minutes later with bowls of hot noodles. His name was Chi-ch'eng. He was sixty-one, and he had been a monk for more than forty years. Originally from Peking, he had moved to the Sian area in the 1950s with his master Yung-ming. Yung-ming, I learned later, was still alive and serving as the abbot of Tzuen Temple and Big Goose Pagoda in Sian. Chi-ch'eng had moved to Chiawutai in 1981 to take over from the previous abbot. I asked him about the history of Hsingching Temple.

Chi-ch'eng: It was first built in the early eighth century. About a hundred years later, Tsung-mi, the Fifth Patriarch of the Huayen school, came here and used his magical powers to bring building materials up the back side of the mountain to enlarge the shrine halls. The temple used to be very imposing, but it was destroyed during the Cultural Revolution. Over the centuries many great monks have lived here.

Q: Do you live here alone?

Chi-ch'eng: No, three other monks also live here. They're not here today. They went down the mountain for provisions.

Chi-ch'eng at the back gate of Hsingching Temple.

Q: What sort of practice do you follow? Do you chant the name of the Buddha or meditate?

Chi-ch'eng: I just pass the time.

Q: Why here?

Chi-ch'eng: Ever since I was young, I've preferred quiet, and I've always loved mountains. I don't like the flatlands. I've also lived in the mountains south of here and in the mountains to the east near Huashan. That was when Yung-ming was head of the Buddhist association in Weinan.

Q: Are there any other monks living near here?

Chi-ch'eng: There was a fifty-year-old monk who moved into Kuanyin Cave two years ago, but he went back to Fukien recently and hasn't returned.

Q: We passed your gardens on our way up the back way. In one of them, we saw the footprint of a wild animal.

Chi-ch'eng: It must have been a wild pig or a tiger. But tigers usually stay in the mountains south of here. They don't come here very often. They used to, but not anymore.

Q: Are there hermits in the mountains south of here?

Chi-ch'eng: Yes, but I only know of a couple. There's one on the other side of Kuanyin Cave. There's a cave on the peak to the west. The nun T'ien-jan moved up there when she was thirty-five and stayed there for fifty years, until she died in 1919. But no one is living there now.

Q: Do you have any plans to repair this temple or add to it?

Chi-ch'eng: Yes, but that will have to wait until conditions improve. Perhaps when our lay supporters are better off, we'll fix both wings and repair the two shrine halls. Poshan Temple down below once housed as many as fifty monks. Except for a small shrine, it's in ruins now. I'd like to help fix it up too.

Q: Is it very windy here?

Chi-ch'eng: Yes, especially in winter. Sometimes the wind blows off the roof tiles. The tiles used to be made of iron.

Q: I imagine it's quiet here as well.

Chi-ch'eng: If people are quiet, they can be quiet anywhere. If people aren't quiet, they won't be quiet here. Everything depends on you. Life is transient, like a flash of lightning or a dream. Eighty years pass like a cloud. We're born, and then we die. But before we receive this form, we had another face, our original face. We can't see it with our eyes. We can only know it with our wisdom. The sutras say, "That which is beyond form is the buddha." We all have the buddha nature. We're all destined to become buddhas. But buddhahood isn't something that can be achieved in a couple of days. You have to practice before you can become aware of your original nature, your original face.

Q: When people visit, do you teach them the Dharma?

Chi-ch'eng: That depends. Everyone's different. To teach, you have to understand what's in the other person's heart, and you have to have some ability. If someone is drowning, and you can't swim, it doesn't do any good to jump in yourself. And if a person doesn't want to be saved, you can't save him. He has to want to be saved.

As he said this, the last rays of sunlight illuminated his face. Steve and I realized it was time to leave. We thanked Chi-ch'eng for the noodles and for his offer to return for a longer stay. He saw us off at the temple gate and went back inside. A minute later, he reemerged with several lanterns. But we had already started down and yelled back that we could make it without them. We waved good-bye, then flew down the steps and past the place where I now stood six months later.

This time, I headed up alone, past the ruins of several small temples, up Cloud Ladder to the cleft boulder that lent its name to Poshan Temple. I looked inside the gate and was surprised to see Chi-ch'eng.

Hsingching Temple at the summit of Chiawutai.

He smiled and said he was taking care of Poshan Temple for the nun who normally lived there. She was due back the next day. He said he had just finished dinner, then went back into the kitchen and heated up some leftover corn gruel and potatoes.

I was hungrier than I'd thought and didn't leave anything for the watchdog who had nearly taken off my leg on the way in. Afterward, Chi-ch'eng took me down a stone staircase just outside the kitchen. It led down the western side of the cliff and across a plank bridge to Lama Cave. He showed me a Tibetan mantra written on the wall by a famous lama who had lived there a hundred years before. He said the monk who currently occupied the cave was in Sian. On the cliff, there was an inscription extolling Chiawutai's seclusion. It was written by a monk named Hsing-k'ung and dated 627, indicating that this was a place of practice at least two hundred years before Tsung-mi came here.

Next to Lama Cave, Chi-ch'eng also showed me Hsiuchenpao Cave. It was like looking inside the night. He said it was for old practitioners who had their own light. On the way back up, he showed me how the plank bridge could be raised, making access to both caves impossible.

The sun went down, and Chi-ch'eng told me to climb the stone ladder called Stairway to Heaven. It took me back up to Hsingching Temple, where I shared his disciple's bed for the night. His disciple was a twenty-year-old novice. He hadn't been ordained, but he had already lived on the mountain for two years and said he liked living on the edge of life. There was plenty of room for both of us on his *k'ang,* but it was April and too late in the year to be lighting the *kang*'s oven. Still, it was cold, and once I settled under the covers, I didn't move until dawn, when I heard birds calling from the next ridge.

At least I didn't have to get dressed. I put on my shoes and walked out the temple's back gate. After crossing the summit's dragon spine, I stopped where a trail led down past a couple of overgrown stupas and back up to the adjacent peak of Hsuehhuashan a hundred meters to the west. I could see part of the stone hut where T'ien-jan had lived for fifty years at the turn of the last century. I bypassed the trail to her hut and continued for another fifty meters, until the trail forked again. The main trail continued past Kuanyin Cave and eventually disappeared down the back side of Chiawutai. I took the other trail and thirty meters later arrived at Tsung-mi's former residence, Wuhua Cave (*Wuhua* being short for "Fifth Patriarch of the Huayen school"). It consisted of a wall of stones piled in front of an overhang. A slate roof where the hut extended beyond the overhang had fallen in. The door faced east and looked out toward the summit of Taihsingshan, ten kilometers to the southeast, where the sun was just rising.

I returned to Hsingching Temple and climbed back down the Stairway to Heaven to Poshan Temple. Chi-ch'eng was stoking the fire in the kitchen and chanting. He said monks who lived in temples ate food prepared by others, but mountain monks had to do everything themselves. I watched him make cornmeal gruel, thinking I might need to know how, myself, someday. He waited for the water to boil, tossed in a dash of arrowroot and then a few handfuls of cornmeal.

Chi-ch'eng said monks who lived in temples had an easy life. They received 50 to 60 RMB (about ten dollars) per month for their personal needs. He laughed and said Yung-ming had been trying to get him to move back down to Big Goose Pagoda. He said he didn't like the flatlands and had no intention of trading the mountains for money. He said, "I didn't become a monk for money or a soft life. I had another purpose. Ever since I was a child, hardships haven't bothered me. I was born to suffer. Monks nowadays aren't the same as before. Those two monks who moved to the back side of Chiawutai won't last one winter. Just because you're a monk doesn't mean you're a buddha. A lot of monks have to wait in line behind a lot of ordinary people for enlightenment. Of course, I shouldn't say this."

While he was talking, the gruel boiled over, and the watchdog was invited in to clean it up. Chi-ch'eng continued, "It doesn't make any difference if you're a monk or a layman, as long as you're not troubled by desire, as long as your mind is unaffected by illusions. Once your mind is clear, you can understand karma. You know what that means? If you plant a buddha-seed, you get a buddha-fruit. The important thing is to be honest. If you're not honest, you'll never succeed. I'm just a mountain man, you know. I just string words together. They don't necessarily make any sense. How about some hot peppers in your potatoes?"

Chapter Eight

The Bird
That Is
a Mountain

*I*n ancient China, every direction had its own spirit: Blue Dragon for the east, Black Turtlesnake for the north, White Tiger for the west, Red Bird for the south. The earliest usage I've been able to find for any of these terms is in the *Shanhaiching*, where the two Chinese characters for Red Bird are combined into one character that refers to a huge red-winged, man-faced owl. Although the origin of these names is unknown, they were in general use as early as the Han dynasty two thousand years ago and were later extended to objects associated with their respective directions.

By the T'ang dynasty six hundred years later, windows that faced south were called "red bird" windows, and gates that faced south were called "red bird" gates. In Ch'ang-an, the palace's Red Bird Gate looked out across a city of 2 million people to the blue ridges of the Chungnan Mountains twenty-five kilometers away. From Red Bird Gate, mountain-bound travelers proceeded down Red Bird Street. It was the city's major north-south thoroughfare and the address of many of its richest and most powerful families. It was also the location of some of the city's most famous landmarks, the first of which was Hsiaoyenta, or Little Goose Pagoda. The pagoda was one and a half kilometers south of Red Bird Gate, and it was the legacy of Yi-ching, Ch'ang-an's second most famous traveler.

As Hsuan-tsang had done fifty years before him, Yi-ching went to India. He left in 671 at the age of thirty-six. But unlike Hsuan-tsang, who took the Silk Road, Yi-ching traveled by sea. And unlike Hsuan-tsang, who went to India for a better understanding of Buddhist philosophy, Yi-ching was more interested in discipline and practice. When he returned twenty-four years later in 695, he was welcomed back by the Empress Dowager Wu Tse-t'ien at the new capital in Loyang. When the court moved back to Ch'ang-an in 705, Yi-ching moved too, to Ch'ang-an's Chienfu Temple on the west side of Red Bird Street.

Again, as Hsuan-tsang had done before him, Yi-ching built a pagoda to safeguard the sutras he brought back. In 706, he built a forty-five-meter tower in the ward south of Chienfu Temple, and it has stood there ever since. In 1965, workers excavating the pagoda's base to make sure it had sufficient support discovered why it had been able to withstand earthquakes that had leveled the surrounding buildings: it was built like a round-bottomed doll that rolls back and then returns to its original position. But while the pagoda has survived, its function as a religious site has not. Government officials are now in charge, and I only stayed long enough to catch my breath beneath the temple's thirteen-hundred-year-old locust trees before returning to the sites of Red Bird Street.

Another kilometer south of Little Goose Pagoda, I parked my bicycle outside the gate of Tahsingshan Temple. Constructed at the end of the third century, it was among the first Buddhist temples built in China. In the seventh century, it was expanded by Emperor Wen of the Sui dynasty into the biggest of the capital's forty-odd temples — occupying a whole ward. And a century later, it was here that Tantric Buddhism first appeared in China. This was where most foreign monks stayed, and in the eighth century the Indian monks Shubhakarasimha, Vajrabodhi, and Amoghavajra all made Tahsingshan Temple their home. All three served as religious instructors to a series of T'ang dynasty emperors, and one of Amoghavajra's students also taught Kukai, the Japanese monk responsible for establishing Tantric Buddhism in Japan.

Tantric Buddhism may have been new to the Chinese, but the individual practices were not so different from many of those already in use—repetition of mystic formulas, channeling of psychic energy, visualization of universal representations, sexual union to augment regular forms of yoga, and the exercise of magic powers. Apparently, Tantric Buddhism's success depended largely on the charisma of its early teachers, rather than on its techniques and doctrines. And when these early teachers died, the interest of the court returned to Taoism and other forms of Buddhism.

Today, Tahsingshan's Tantric past is all but forgotten, and its function as a place of practice is overshadowed by its use as a hostel for visiting monks and as headquarters for the Shensi Buddhist Association. During one of my visits, I talked with the association's director, Layman Hsu Li. Hsu had spent several decades as a monk but was forced to return to lay life during the Cultural Revolution. Despite the government's new policy guaranteeing religious freedom, he has remained a layman.

Through an intermediary, we agreed to meet at the temple, but at the last minute, I canceled. His assistant later told me that at the originally appointed time, three security agents had arrived at Hsu's door and stood outside for several hours, until it became clear I wasn't coming. Several days later, I arranged an appointment by more circuitous means, and we met in his room without any outside interference. I asked him how many monks and nuns lived in Shensi Province.

Hsu: I have no idea. Monks and nuns can come and go at will and stay wherever there's room. We don't keep statistics. If we did, every monk would probably get counted four or five times. Also, nowadays younger monks might live in a monastery for a while, then go back home for a while, and then return to the monastery again. Sometimes it's hard to say whether they're really monks. Not so many people enter monasteries anymore with the idea of staying for the rest of their lives.

Q: What about hermits? I understand many monks and nuns spend part of their lives practicing by themselves in the Chungnan Mountains.

Hsu: I don't know how many hermits there are either. There have been hermits in the Chungnan Mountains for at least three thousand years. But there are different kinds of hermits: Taoist hermits, Buddhist hermits, and intellectual hermits. Of course, I'm more familiar with Buddhist hermits. But even in Buddhism there are different kinds of hermits. Pure Land hermits, for example, usually spend their lives in the mountains, while Zen hermits might spend only a few years or months. Zen hermits only stay in the mountains until they find the Way, then they come down.

But before they become hermits, monks and nuns usually spend several years in a monastery. Many monks, for example, go to Kaoming Temple in Yangchou and practice there for three or four years. When they finally begin to get somewhere in their practice, they go live in a mountain hut for another three or four years. Sooner or later they become enlightened. Some take longer than others. But first, you have to live in a monastery and study. You have to study before you know how to practice.

In Buddhist monasteries we also have a custom called *pi-kuan* [enclosure]. Yin-kuang, for example, lived in an enclosure on Puto Island for several decades. [Yin-kuang was the monk responsible for the renaissance of Pure Land practice in the twentieth century.] For several decades he didn't see anyone. Every day the monks at the temple slipped food and water through a slot in his door and emptied his chamber pot. All he did was meditate and read sutras. You don't have to go to the mountains to practice.

There are also intellectual hermits. They prefer quiet and seclusion in order to study or write. Many people have lived in the Chungnan Mountains as hermits, some for social reasons, some for religious reasons, some for intellectual reasons.

Q: If a monk or nun wants to live in this province as a hermit, do they need to register with the association or gain its approval?

Hsu: No, anyone who wants to be a hermit is free to do so. They don't need to tell us or the government. They can live wherever they want.

Q: What purpose does the association serve?

Hsu: We represent the temples in the province in dealing with the government. We also provide advice to monks and nuns on how to organize their religious activities, what activities are acceptable, and where such activities are allowed. China has had Buddhist associations since ancient times; Taoist associations too. Every county and every province had a special temple in charge of religious affairs, and there was one for the whole country. Now we use the word *association,* but the function hasn't changed. We take care of religious affairs that are too big for a single temple or help solve other problems that occur.

Q: Whom do the temples belong to?

Hsu: They belong to the committees that run them. A temple committee can include anywhere from two or three people up to two or three hundred. The committee decides how to raise and distribute funds, whether to repair the temple or buy new blankets, that sort of thing. Anyone who lives in a temple becomes a member of the committee. Every temple runs its own affairs. The association doesn't get involved unless we're asked to help solve a problem.

Q: Is Buddhism taught in schools?

Hsu: It's not taught in elementary school or high school, but there are several universities with courses in Buddhism. We used to have classes. But we were forced to stop. Recently many people have asked me to begin classes again. As soon as we can arrange funding for books and materials, we plan to start. Almost every province has some sort of Buddhist academy. I think there are more than twenty now. We don't have one in Shensi yet, but we hope to in the future.

My meeting with Hsu Li was in September of 1989. In late March of the following year, I visited Tahsingshan Temple again. Inside the rear shrine hall, past several bushes of late-blooming plum flowers, a profusion of forsythia, and an ancient grapevine getting ready for summer, I met Hui-yu, the temple's abbot. He was seventy-eight and had been living at the temple since coming from Honan Province forty years earlier. He had been a monk for fifty years. Although he used a cane in concession to a bad knee, he was energetic and hardly in need of the several disciples who hovered around him. He said that twenty monks lived at the temple permanently, although visiting monks often increased the number to a hundred.

Hui-yu's eyelids were only half-open, suggesting he spent a lot of time meditating. And he laughed a lot. I thought he might be a Zen monk, but he talked about Pure Land practice instead. He said there were still enlightened masters in China but not as many as before. Unfortunately, he had to attend a meeting and our talk was brief. But before his disciples hurried him off, he suggested I visit the hermits on Nanwutai, which was where mountain-bound travelers on Red Bird Street usually ended up in the old days. I thanked him and headed for the main gate.

On my way out the previous September, I had stopped to watch a demonstration of shamanistic healing by the Shensi Ch'i-Kung Association. The association rented a building from the temple for use as a clinic as well as for its provincial headquarters. Inside, a young man dressed in a white laboratory coat was walking around a woman. Her eyes were closed, and she was spinning wildly, moaning and shouting. The man gestured with his hands, as if he were controlling her movements. I watched for about twenty minutes, but it seemed like it would never end, so I left.

It was six months later, and this time I decided to stop in for a treatment. Since returning to China, I had developed a rash on my arms that had resisted the various pills and ointments prescribed by two regular doctors. I registered and paid the rather steep treatment fee of 30 RMB, or six dollars.

The doctor's name was Ho Chien-hsin. In addition to treating patients, he served as director of China's national *ch'i-kung* troupe, which toured other countries, amazing audiences with the abilities that cultivation of *ch'i* made possible, *ch'i* being the energy that is empty both in the body and in the world. After feeling my various pulses, he said the rash was nothing more than exposure to wind. He told me to stand with my legs apart and my eyes closed; then he started walking around me humming and making sloshing and whooshing sounds with the movement of the *ch'i* inside his body. After a few minutes of this, he told me to sit down and started sticking acupuncture needles into my body, between my thumbs and index fingers, in the nape of my neck, in my arms, in my knees, and in my ankles. Then he told me to close my eyes and to breathe out, as if I were a punctured tire.

While I sat there leaking air, he treated other patients and occasionally returned to twirl the needles and to shout and slosh his *ch'i* around. Finally, he prescribed an herbal medicine. Two days later, the rash was gone.

Meanwhile, I decided to take Hui-yu's advice. I exchanged my bicycle for a car and driver and headed for Nanwutai on Red Bird Street's present incarnation as Ch'ang-an Road, a hundred meters east of its ancient counterpart.

Two kilometers south of Tahsingshan Temple, we stopped at the well-kept grave of General Yang Hu-ch'eng. Yang had liberated and then defended Sian from local warlords in the 1920s and later had assisted in the arrest of his own commander-in-chief, Chiang Kai-shek. In ancient times, travelers stopped here to visit Niutou Temple. But it was gone. They also stopped to visit a memorial shrine to China's greatest poet, Tu Fu.

Tu Fu was born in 712 in the neighboring province of Honan. But the Shaoling Plateau south of Ch'ang-an was his ancestral home, and he later spent his most productive years here. In fact, he called himself the "recluse of Shaoling" and titled his collected poems after this area. He died in 770, while wandering south of the Yangtze, and was buried near Changsha in Hunan Province. About a hundred years after his death, someone built a shrine here to his memory, and it's been rebuilt a number of times since then.

I climbed the slope behind General Yang's grave to visit the present version of the shrine. It was built in 1960, but it had already been abandoned to weeds and chickens. In a side building, I found the caretaker chopping vegetables. He came out and unlocked the shrine hall. In the middle of an otherwise empty hall was a dusty plaster statue of Tu Fu holding the jade tablet of a court official he never held while alive. There was an even dustier portrait carved in stone, and everywhere were spider webs.

Outside, along one of the crumbling corridors, I read several of the steles commemorating the shrine's renovations in the Ming and Ch'ing dynasties. Apparently, every two hundred years or so, somebody got the idea of resurrecting this shrine, but obviously, such attention was short-lived. Generals fared better than the country's greatest poet.

Continuing south, we stopped again after another kilometer. Behind a school and just below the western edge of the Shaoling Plateau were two pagodas, the last traces of Huayen Temple. The temple was first built around 630 and was the residence of the series of patriarchs who founded the Huayen school of Chinese Buddhism: Tu-shun, Chih-yen, Fa-tsang, Ch'ih-liang, and, finally, Tsung-mi, the fifth and last patriarch of this school.

The teaching of this school was based on the *Avatamsaka*, or *Huayen, Sutra.* According to Buddhist legend, this was the Buddha's first sermon following his Enlightenment. When his audience failed to understand its message, the Buddha put it aside in favor of simpler teachings. The central teaching of this sutra is that everything in the universe, whether noumenon or phenomenon, is interconnected and thus empty of any self-nature. And empty of self-nature, everything is thus one with the Dharma, everyone is one with the Buddha.

To illustrate this, the third patriarch once set up a buddha figure and surrounded it with mirrors on all sides as well as above and below. Not only was the figure reflected in each mirror, each mirror also reflected the images of the other mirrors, ad infinitum. Imagine a buddha wherever you look.

It was an elegant philosophy. But the persecution of Buddhism in 844, three years after the death of Tsung-mi, brought an end to the Huayen lineage. A thousand years later, the edge of the plateau collapsed and swept away any structures that remained, except for two brick pagodas containing the remains of the first and fourth patriarchs. I was told that plans were under way to rebuild the temple, but I saw no signs that anyone but farmers and ravens visited the site.

I slid back down the plateau, returned to the car, and continued heading south. After seven kilometers, the road forked left to Hsing-chiao Temple and right to Nanwutai. We headed toward the blue peaks of Nanwutai and followed the road west.

Six kilometers past the fork, we passed another road to the left. It led to the village of Taiyikung, named for a temple built in the Han dynasty by Emperor Wu. The emperor often came here to pay his respects to T'ai-yi, the highest god in the Taoist pantheon in those days. The temple was long gone, and the road, which led south into Taiyi Gorge and part way up Tsuihuashan, was now lined by military installations. We stayed on the main road.

After three kilometers, we turned south at the village of Nanwutai and continued for one more kilometer to Mito Temple at the foot of the mountain. It was a confusion of buildings, suggesting a confused past. As we entered, I couldn't help noticing a huge, ancient magnolia blooming next to the front shrine hall. Another grew in the courtyard behind it. Together they blanketed the hall with white petals and a subtle fragrance. The shrine hall itself was completely taken up by a garish plaster statue of Maitreya, the buddha destined to follow Shakyamuni. It begged for the return of the Red Guards.

The rear shrine hall was a welcome contrast. Instead of the usual altar or statue, a pagoda dominated the center of the hall. And lining the pagoda and all the walls were stone carvings of five hundred Buddhist worthies. The workmanship was superb. I later learned that Buddhists in Hong Kong had hired eight stone-carvers from the southern coastal city of Swatow to do the work, and it had taken them two years. Among the statues lining the pagoda were my old friends Han-shan (Cold Mountain) and Shih-te (Pickup).

I was so impressed with the carvings, I almost overlooked the thousands of magnolia sepals, or flower casings, covering the floor. Later, the abbot told me that as soon as the weather improved, the monks planned to dry them outside and sell them for use in a medicine for sinusitis.

Out in the courtyard, I poked my head inside one of the side rooms and saw the abbot, whom I had met six months before. As soon as he saw me, he laughed. I never met a monk who laughed more. I don't think he ever said more than two or three sentences without stopping to chuckle. His name was Te-ch'eng. He was sixty-nine, and he had grown up as a farmer in Ch'ang-an County. He became a monk when he was thirty, and after studying in a temple for several years, he became a hermit on the summit of Kuanyinshan, up the Feng River gorge. After six years, he moved to Chingyeh Temple near the mouth of the gorge and eventually served as abbot of both Chingyeh Temple and nearby Fengte Temple. He said that before the Cultural Revolution, there were forty monks at Chingyeh Temple and sixty nuns at Fengte Temple and hermits in many of the forty-eight huts in Tung-kou Gully.

In 1985, the provincial Buddhist association asked Te-ch'eng to take over Mito Temple. He said that when he arrived, there was nothing—no monks, no shrine halls, nothing. The shrine halls had been destroyed during the Cultural Revolution, and the remaining buildings had been occupied by government officials and soldiers. Somehow he got them all to move out. Judging from his nearly constant chuckle, I'm sure it wasn't through confrontation. I asked him what he taught people who came to him for instruction, and his answer was punctuated by frequent laughter.

Te-ch'eng: I teach all sorts of odds and ends. You name it. Whatever seems to fit. A little of this, a little of that. This is what practice is all about. You can't practice just one kind of dharma. That's a mistake. The Dharma isn't one-sided. You have to practice Zen. If you don't, you'll never break through delusions. And you've got to practice the precepts. If you don't, your life will be a mess. And you've got to practice Pure Land. If you don't, you'll never get any help from the Buddha. You have to practice all dharmas.

It's like making a fire. You need more than a spark. You need wood and air too. If one of them is missing, you can't make fire. It's the same with enlightenment. It's a system. All practices are related. You can't leave one of them out. The mind encompasses everything. You can't leave anything out. You can't have anything outside the mind. The mind has to be one. There's only room for one thought, no delusions, nothing else. In Zen, you have no thought. In Pure Land, you have one thought. They're both the same. They're both aimed at showing you who you are.

We also talked about the Chungnan Mountains. Like the abbot of Hsiangchi Temple and Taiwan's Professor Tu Er-wei, Te-ch'eng was of the opinion that the Chungnan Mountains stretched all the way to India. He found that funny too. I would have talked with him longer, but I was tired and yawned. He suggested I go to bed, and after I sent the car and driver back to Sian he led me to a room occupied by one of his disciples.

The disciple was a monk by the name of Hsing-k'ung. He was twenty-eight, and he moved with the grace of a young girl. On the table next to his bed was a white porcelain bust of Mao Tse-tung. I couldn't help but wonder what it was doing in a monastery. He saw me staring at it, and he told me his parents had been high-ranking party cadres. They died while he was young, in the middle of the Cultural Revolution, and he was raised by relatives. After graduating from Peking University, he started working for the government in an international trading unit. He had traveled to America and Canada and Europe. He was the first monk I had met who could speak some English.

He said that one day two years ago he visited Mito Temple with some friends and ended up spending the night. During the night, Kuan-yin, the Bodhisattva of Compassion, appeared to him in a dream and taught him the Dharma. The next morning, he told his friends to go back to Peking without him.

When he stepped out of the room for a few minutes, a laywoman who had brought me a bowl of noodles whispered that Hsing-k'ung was no ordinary monk. He had special powers. He was a living buddha. She said that in the two years since he had been at the temple, he had cured over five thousand people through faith in the scriptures. She left as soon as Hsing-k'ung returned, and I fell asleep in a matter of minutes. Instead of Kuan-yin, all I heard that night was the sound of rats chasing each other.

The next morning after breakfast, Hsing-k'ung showed me a chest full of robes he had been making for all the hermits in the area. There must have been fifty robes, all different colors—one was even emerald green. He said he bought the material with money left by people he had cured. Then he said that patients would be lining up outside his door in a few minutes and suggested I leave. But first, he gave me election receipts to give several of the monks and nuns who lived along the trail that led up Nanwutai. They had all chosen Hsing-k'ung as their representative in the local village council.

I said good-bye and started up Taikou Gorge on the trail that began just outside the temple. The temperature had dropped below freezing during the night, and the gorge was half-veiled in fog. All I could see were the stone steps. After about two kilometers, I arrived at Wufo Temple. Two ancient locust trees guarded the front.

Inside the temple, I talked with two seventy-year-old monks, Ch'uan-hsin and Fa-yi. But I had trouble understanding their dialect, and we did little more than exchange introductions. I gave them their election receipts, and they showed me some steps behind the temple.

The steps led up a slope covered with fir trees recently planted by the forest service. After about three hundred meters, the steps ended halfway up the slope at what remained of Paita Cemetery. The name means "hundred stupas," but the only stupa still standing was that of Yin-kuang. Yin-kuang is ranked, along with Hsu-yun, as one of the greatest monks of this century. While Hsu-yun renewed the practice of Zen in China, Yin-kuang did the same for Pure Land practice. People who attended his sermons say they were never the same afterward. His stupa was empty, his remains having been removed from its interior. Over the opening was his name, written by Yu Yu-jen, China's most celebrated calligrapher of the twentieth century. Yu's own grave was just over the hill from where I lived in Taiwan.

Surrounding the stupa was a grove of deciduous pines, a present from Japan's Prime Minister Tanaka. In the fifteen years since they had been planted, they had already grown to about eight meters. To the

Yin-kuang's stupa.

south, just beyond the stand of pines, was the huge pagoda that had established the site as a cemetery at the end of the sixth century. It was the first of the Sian area's giant pagodas, predating by fifty years Hsuan-tsang's Big Goose Pagoda. Next to the pagoda was Shengshou Temple, where I talked briefly with one of the two resident monks. Inside, leaning against one of the walls, were the two halves of the cracked stone-carving of Yin-kuang that had once covered the opening of his stupa.

I returned to the main trail and for the next two hours passed ruin after ruin. Nanwutai is situated directly south of Ch'ang-an, and it had become the area's major Buddhist center as early as the Sui and T'ang dynasties, and was still flourishing as late as the Ming and Ch'ing dynasties. At the turn of the last century, there were still seventy-two temples and shrines along the trail to the summit. Now only five remain—and all of them newly rebuilt. Everything standing when the Cultural Revolution swept China in the 1960s was destroyed by the Red Guards.

Just beyond Wufo Temple, the trail climbed away from the gorge and crossed a road opened by the forest service about the same time the Red Guards began destroying temples. The first time I came here, with Steve, we had driven up. This time, I stayed on the trail and crossed the road several more times before finally reaching the parking lot and going up the same stone steps Steve and I and our driver had climbed six months earlier.

After about fifty meters, I passed Fire Dragon Cave. It was once the home of a dragon that periodically terrorized Ch'ang-an until Kuan-yin caught him, put him in Dragon Cage farther up the mountain, ground him into powder, and threw the powder into the Wei River.

Except for a small shrine, the cave was empty, and I continued on. A few minutes later, something roared and I froze. I suddenly remembered that I hadn't lit incense at Fire Dragon Cave. Then I heard the roar again. It wasn't a dragon. But I didn't breathe any easier—it was a bear.

I knew from my last visit that there was a hostel about ten minutes up the trail, and I hurried ahead—slowly, if that's possible. I heard the roar a few more times, but it seemed to be getting fainter. When I finally made it to the hostel, the caretaker said the bear had just left. Probably it had been complaining about the poor quality of the hostel's garbage. Weeds were everywhere. And, except for the caretaker, the place was deserted. It had recently been built on what remained of the summer residence of Liu Lan-t'ao. Before the Cultural Revolution branded him as a Capitalist Roader, Liu was the Communist Party's secretary-general for the country's five northwest provinces and one of the most powerful men in the country. I congratulated Liu on his choice of scenery.

I gave the bear enough time to clear out, then resumed my hike up the trail. After another kilometer or so, I stopped at Tzuchulin Temple. When Steve and I had hiked up the previous fall, a number of young monks had been rebuilding the trail outside the front gate. The abbot had given us slices of watermelon and complained about the number of tourists who came to climb the peak.

This time, there were still traces of snow, and I was the only tourist on the mountain. The abbot welcomed me back. His name was Yen-ch'eng. He was sixty-six, and he lived at the temple with three other monks and several laymen. Before coming to Nanwutai, he had lived in a hut sixty kilometers to the west up the Kung River gorge. The first time I hiked up Nanwutai with Steve, our driver had stayed behind to listen to Yen-ch'eng explain what he and the other monks were doing on the mountain. I asked Yen-ch'eng what he had told our driver.

Yen-ch'eng: I talked about meditation. I explained how we first chant the name of the Buddha to settle the mind. Only when the mind is settled can it become quiet. Then I explained how we quiet the mind by asking who's chanting the name of the Buddha. Only when the mind is quiet can it become still. Then I explained how we still the mind by putting aside the name of the Buddha. Only when the mind is still can it see. And only when the mind can see can it reach the mystery of mysteries. I explained that this is a process that anyone who practices has to go through. How long it takes is up to the individual. It's like walking down a road. The road keeps changing. Sometimes it's easy, sometimes it's hard. But for people who practice, living in the mountains is much easier than living in the city. Our life looks hard to outsiders, but we're not concerned with comfort. We're here to practice. And practice has no form. Most visitors think we're just poor monks.

The fog made the time seem later than it was, and I stayed only long enough to share a cup of tea and a plate of deep-fried twists of dough and to take a picture for Yen-ch'eng of his master's stupa, one of three remaining in the temple's cemetery.

Then I walked on for another thirty minutes. Three side trails on the left led to the five nearby peaks that make up Nanwutai's summit — and from which the mountain takes its name: Five Platforms of the South.

The highest of the five has an elevation slightly under 2,400 meters and is called Tating or Kuanyintai. One of the first temples built in this part of the Chungnan Mountains was built on Tating in the Sui dynasty. It was called Yuankuang Temple. During Kao Ho-nien's last visit to Nanwutai during the winter and spring of 1914–1915, he watched from Dragon Cage while Yuankuang Temple burned, the result of too many candles or too much incense. The sight reminded Kao of the transience of life and our efforts to build something permanent. Better to build an empty mind.

The fog was so thick, I couldn't see more than a few meters and decided to pass up going to the peaks. Instead, I continued on, crossed the ridge, and headed down the other side. Ten minutes later, I arrived at the gate of Tamaopeng. Like all the other temples on the mountain, Tamaopeng had been recently rebuilt — and had seen better days. When it was first built in the sixth century, it was called Hsi-lin Temple. Later, it became a meeting place for all the hermits on the mountain, and people started calling it Tamaopeng, or Big Hut.

During my first visit, I had met the temple's abbot, Te-san. He was seventy-four years old and from Peking. When he was still a child, his father lost his job and asked the monks at Peking's Kuangchi Temple to take care of his son. Te-san was ten when he became a novice. When he was old enough to become a monk, he traveled south and studied at Buddhist academies in Ningpo and Canton. Afterward, he traveled all over China studying with various masters and establishing a number of Buddhist academies himself. He came to the Chungnan Mountains late in life, in 1985. He said he didn't plan to move again. I asked him why he chose this area.

Te-san: The most important thing for a monk is spiritual practice, and for this he needs a quiet place. This mountain is quiet. In China we have a number of mountains where most monks go for practice. This is one of them. It's a place where monks and nuns practice by themselves. Ever since the T'ang dynasty, this area has been a center for those who want to concentrate on religious practice.

Q: What about now?

Te-san: Ever since the new religious policy was announced by the government ten years ago, religious activities have resumed just about everywhere. There aren't as many monks as there used to be, but things are getting better.

Q: What about here?

Te-san: A lot of monks and nuns come here to visit but not many stay. There are only four of us here. Except for the morning and evening ceremonies in the shrine hall, we all practice on our own.

Q: How do you support yourselves?

Te-san: Lay Buddhists in Sian and Shanghai have been helping us. We don't have any problems in this respect.

Q: Are there many hermits on Nanwutai?

Te-san: There aren't as many as there used to be. When I visited Nanwutai in the 1950s, there were more than seventy monks and nuns living in huts on this side of the mountain [the south side]. Now there are only a dozen or so.

Q: Does the government mind?

Te-san: No. As long as they register with the Buddhist association in Sian, they can live wherever they want. [See Layman Hsu's comment about this on p. 152.]

Q: How do they support themselves?

Te-san: They plant vegetables and gather firewood. For other necessities, most of them rely on lay people or relatives.

Q: Are you bothered by visitors here?

Te-san: No, not many people visit this mountain. It takes them too long to get here from Sian. By that time, they have to go back. Besides, we don't sell entrance tickets like some temples do. People can come here to worship but not as tourists.

Q: What sort of practice do you cultivate?

Te-san: Zen. We follow the teachings of Zen. Most of the monks who come here have lived in larger temples and have practiced group meditation. Here we meditate on our own. When one of the monks has a problem or a question, he asks me, and I try to help him. That's all.

Q: Can anyone stay here?

Te-san: Normally, they have to be introduced by someone we know. After that, they have to undergo a period of training to see if a monk's life really suits them before we can accept them as disciples.

Q: Is the understanding of new disciples more superficial than before?

Te-san: Yes, but people can learn. The real problem is that there aren't very many monks my age around to teach them. To penetrate the most profound teachings of the Buddha, disciples need a teacher who has a great deal of experience and learning. This is especially true for Zen.

This time when I visited Tamaopeng, Te-san was gone. He was in a hospital in Sian and not expected to return. One of his disciples had taken charge of the temple. His name was Pao-sheng. He was forty-four, and he shared the temple with two other monks, both of whom had gone to Sian for a few days to see Te-san. There was also a monk visiting from Chekiang Province. Before the Cultural Revolution, more than fifty monks lived at Tamaopeng.

After introductions and a cup of tea, Pao-sheng invited me to spend the night. I gladly accepted but said I'd be back in a few hours. I wanted to visit Hui-yuan, a nun I had met six months earlier.

When he visited Nanwutai, Kao Ho-nien also stayed at Tamaopeng and made day trips to the peaks and surrounding huts. During one trip, he took the same trail that I was taking and visited hermits at Hsiangtzu Cave, Tiger's Lair, and Dragon Cage.

I also stopped at Hsiangtzu Cave, a few hundred meters past Tamaopeng. This was where the Taoist immortal Han Hsiang-tzu lived in the T'ang dynasty. Now a Buddhist layman was living inside, but he was oblivious to anything but the Buddha's name, so I continued down the trail. I soon passed the ruins of Dragon Cage, and then the trail forked. The main trail went to Taiyi Gorge and Tsuihua-shan, where half a dozen monks were reportedly living at Tienchih Temple. The trail on the right led to Hui-yuan's hut.

As I hiked down through the fog, a bird flew by—its body a flash of blue and white, its tail completely black. All around me was swirling mist, and all I could see was the trail. In August, the vegetation had been so lush, it seemed almost tropical. Now it was all decaying leaves and black branches. Finally, after about thirty minutes, I arrived at Hui-yuan's hut. It was called Hsiaomaopeng, or Little Hut, to distinguish it from Tamaopeng, and Chingtu Maopeng, to distinguish it as a place of Pure Land practice.

The first time Steve and I visited, the gate was locked, and we had to wait five minutes for Hui-yuan's disciple to come down and open it. This time, the gate stood wide open. I was surprised. Six months earlier, I walked through the most beautiful garden of vegetables and flowers I'd seen anywhere in the mountains. Now it was late March, foggy, and below freezing. The only signs of life were buds on the apple trees.

As I approached the hut, I shouted the name of the Buddha. Hui-yuan's disciple appeared in the doorway. Her name was Ch'eng-po. She was thirty-five and had decided to become a nun after visiting Hui-yuan with some friends one day ten years ago. A few months later, she became a nun, and Hui-yuan agreed to accept her as a disciple. She smiled, lifted the white sheet that hung in the doorway, and showed me inside. I was stunned. Leaning against the whitewashed walls of Hui-yuan's shrine room were six government officials. They almost dropped their cigarettes when I walked in. But before any of us could recover, Ch'eng-po whisked me through another curtain into Hui-yuan's bedroom.

Hui-yuan was sitting in bed with her legs crossed under a blanket. Two glass-paned windows let in light, and against the whitewashed adobe walls were calendar scenes and several old photos. Hui-yuan was from Harbin in northeast China. She was seventy-one years old, and she had been a nun since she was sixteen. She came to Nanwutai in 1955 with another nun, Hui-ying. Soon after they arrived, they moved into this hut, which had been vacated by a hermit who moved to Chiawutai. They lived here until the Red Guards came and forced them to leave. After a brief period in the Buddhist work crew down at Mito Temple, they returned and went back to work in their garden, chanting the Buddha's name. Hui-ying died in 1981.

Hui-yuan asked me to join her on her adobe bed. I told her all the hermit news from Chiawutai and the Feng River gorge. Finally, I asked her what the officials were doing in her hut.

Hui-yuan: They just wanted to visit me, to find out if I needed anything. It's the first time this has ever happened. I don't know what it means.

Q: The last time I visited, you told me you hadn't been down the mountain in over ten years. Have you been down recently?

Hui-yuan: No. I don't plan to go down the mountain again. First, I'm too lazy. Second, I'm too ill. I can't walk so far anymore. I don't want to go anywhere. I just eat and sleep and sit here all day.

Q: What do you do when you need to buy things?

Hui-yuan with her disciple, beside her apple tree.

Hui-yuan: I have a sister who works in Canton. She came here once. She sends me money from time to time. I don't need much. I grow my own vegetables, and I use the money she sends me to buy things like flour and cooking oil. My disciple goes down the mountain to bring things up. We don't eat much, just breakfast and lunch. We don't eat supper.

Q: You get mail here?

Hui-yuan: Yes, there's a mailman who goes around the mountain every week or so.

Q: Then you have an address?

Hui-yuan: Yes, Ch'ang-an County, Shihpienyu Township, Chingtu Maopeng.

Q: What sort of practice do you follow?

Hui-yuan: Trying to stay alive keeps me pretty busy. But I get up every day before dawn and chant the *Lotus Sutra* and the *Titsang Sutra*. At night, I meditate and chant the name of the Buddha. Practice depends on the individual. This is my practice.

Q: Why do you live in the mountains?

Hui-yuan: I like quiet. Anyone who becomes a monk or nun prefers quiet. Monks or nuns who can preach live in the city. I can't preach, so I live in the mountains and practice by myself.

Q: How is your health?

Hui-yuan: Not so good. I've worn myself out carrying things up the mountain and clearing this slope to plant vegetables. Last year I started spitting up blood. A laywoman brought a doctor to see me, and he gave me some medicine. I'm better now. But I've had a chronic illness since I was thirty. Now I'm just getting old.

Q: How do you survive the winters?

Hui-yuan: I don't mind the winters. It gets cold outside, but there's enough wood. The wind doesn't come through the door or the windows, and my bed is a *k'ang* [a brick bed with a built-in stove]. I like the winters. They're a good time to meditate.

We shared a pot of tea, and I gave her a picture Steve had taken of her six months earlier next to one of her apple trees. On my way out, I also gave Ch'eng-po their election receipts and some food her mother had asked me to bring down to her. Her mother was staying at Tamaopeng for a few weeks, helping out in the kitchen. I said goodbye and started back up. It was so cold, I didn't even sweat.

Back at Tamaopeng, Pao-sheng cleared off the bed next to his; then Ch'eng-po's mother brought us big bowls of noodles for dinner. Afterward, I curled up under half a dozen cotton blankets and slept. Several times during the night, I rolled over and noticed Pao-sheng sitting up. He spent the entire night meditating. The next morning I asked him about practice.

Along the Nanwutai trail.

Pao-sheng: Some monks chant sutras, some meditate. But you don't have to sit to meditate. When my master got too old and couldn't sit up anymore, he meditated lying down. But just because someone looks like they're meditating doesn't mean they're practicing. You can tell someone who practices. Everything they do and say is to the point. They don't engage in idle talk or idle activities. This isn't just my opinion. This is what Zen masters teach in the meditation hall. I can tell you honestly that those who truly practice are few. As for myself, I don't practice much. I meditate at night and do chores during the day. I'm just taking care of the temple.

Q: Do you know of any other monks or nuns practicing deeper in the mountains?

Pao-sheng: I've heard about several monks living at a place called Tienchih [not the temple of the same name on nearby Tsuihuashan]. I've never been there, and I'm not sure of its location, but I've heard it's up Shihpien Gorge about fifteen kilometers southwest of here. I've heard that several monks are living there in complete seclusion, practicing what we call *pi-kuan* [enclosure]. I'm not sure who's taking care of their needs, maybe some other monks or lay people.

Q: Can you grow enough vegetables to support yourself?

Pao-sheng: That depends. Even when the weather's good, there are so many squirrels and rats and other wild animals, it's hard to grow enough to live on. Many monks and nuns visit these mountains, but not many are able to stay here. It's not easy. Only those who are devoted to their practice can survive here.

Q: How long have you been a monk?

Pao-sheng: I've only been a monk for three years, but I've been practicing for a long time. Many years ago, I sold my house in Sian and moved into a temple. But the abbot treated me very badly.

Still, whenever someone criticizes me, I don't care if it's just or not. I examine myself. But I had so many problems with the abbot, I finally left and moved to Chingliang Maopeng. It's another hour or so past

Hui-yuan's hut. But while I was living there, I became very sick. I must have eaten something poisonous. I became too weak to move, and my whole body swelled up like a balloon. I would have died, but two laymen appeared out of nowhere and nursed me back to health. They must have been bodhisattvas. I never saw them before or after. Later, when I was able to walk, I returned home to Sian to recuperate. For three months, I couldn't eat regular food. After my mother died, I left home again and returned to the mountains. This time I found a good master and studied with him for several years, until he died.

I was impressed by Pao-sheng's sincerity and simplicity and wished more people were as honest with themselves and others as he was. We said good-bye at the temple gate. A few seconds later, he was a figure in black. A few seconds later, he was gone.

I crossed the ridge and worked my way back down the mountain's north slope, past the trails to the fogged-in peaks, past Tzuchulin Temple, past the empty hostel, past Fire Dragon Cave. It was an easy walk, but the heavy mist and freezing cold had made the trail wet and icy. When I reached the parking lot, I decided to take the road the rest of the way down.

Six months before, when Steve and I drove down the same road after sunset, we saw a huge bird perched on a rock at the side of the road. It was blinded by our headlights. We stopped the car, and when I opened the door, it suddenly stretched its wings. They must have had a span of six feet, and they were red. The face we saw blinked and disappeared into the darkness. This time all I saw was the mountain.

Chapter Nine

Crossing
Heartbreak
Bridge

*I*n ancient China, the most heavily traveled road was the one that connected the western capitals of Feng, Hao, Hsienyang, and Ch'ang-an with the eastern capital of Loyang and the central plains. The Loyang Road, as it was called, also skirted the foothills of the Chungnan Mountains, and this was the road many would-be hermits took when they decided to leave Ch'ang-an for good.

I hired a car and from Sian's East Gate followed the road east for ten kilometers to the Pa River. This was the first major obstacle travelers encountered in ancient times. In spring, the Pa River can become as much as half a kilometer wide. Although armies are reported to have crossed the river as early as the middle of the seventh century B.C., the first mention of a bridge in historical records doesn't occur until the third century B.C., when the First Emperor came here to see off one of his generals.

The Pachiao Bridge (*Pachiao* means "Pa bridge") was where everyone who could afford the time came to see off their friends and colleagues heading east. Over the centuries, it also became known as Heartbreak Bridge—the most famous place in ancient China to say good-bye and the backdrop to a million poems about willows.

Until modern times, their hanging catkins lined both shores of the Pa River for several kilometers in either direction. In late spring, the fuzz of the catkins filled the air like snow, creating another of Shensi's eight wonders. In Chinese, the word for "willow" is a homophone for "stay," and those who stayed broke off a catkin to give to those who left. It was the most meaningful of parting gifts and one that everyone could afford. The willows are gone now, cut down several decades ago during a flood control project.

The bridge, or at least a recent version, remains. It was built in 1834 on the same site used since the end of the sixth century A.D. Today, it's used for traffic entering Sian. For cars and buses and trucks and donkey carts heading east out of town, there's a new bridge two kilometers to the south.

In ancient times, many people looking for seclusion stopped right here. Instead of crossing Pachiao Bridge, they settled into the Paling Foothills (*Paling* means "foothills of the Pa") between the bridge and Pailuyuan, or White Deer Plateau to the south.

These foothills were first made famous by Emperor Wen of the Han dynasty, who chose them as his burial site. Emperor Wen was one of those rare rulers who would have been just as happy as a hermit. His preference for simplicity was legendary. He wore straw sandals to court. In his testament, he noted that people of his time spent fortunes constructing elaborate graves and asked that his funeral involve a minimum of display and that his grave not contain anything more valuable than pottery. He was buried at Paling in 157 B.C. in accordance with his wishes.

Just before the bridge, we turned off and headed for his grave. Six kilometers later, we stopped. From the road, White Deer Plateau looked like two wings outstretched and joined to a beak that pointed toward the sky. Emperor Wen's grave was below the beak. A farmer showed me the way.

At the base of the slope was the site of the former shrine. Nine recently unearthed Ming and Ch'ing dynasty steles marked the spot. The farmer said there were more than forty steles before the Red Guards visited the site. They also cut down a cedar planted here when

Emperor Wen was buried. The farmer recalled climbing on its branches when he was young. The grave mound itself was on a knoll beyond the steles about five hundred meters from the river. It was mid-March when I visited and the slopes were covered with the white blossoms of hundreds of apricot trees. Apricots for long life.

I returned to the road, and we drove back toward the bridge. Along the way, we passed several dozen villagers walking in single file. Strips of white cloth were wrapped around their heads and trailed down their backs. It was a funeral procession. One villager at the end of the procession stopped to pee. Just the sort of ceremony Emperor Wen would have appreciated.

Halfway to the bridge, near the village of Maoyaoyuan, I noticed a series of six caves carved into the plateau less than a kilometer from the road. Two of them had been fitted with doors. Farmhouses in the Sian area usually have black doors with a thin line of red trim. These doors were completely red. We stopped, and I scanned them with my binoculars. I saw the name of the Buddha and Buddhist swastikas on strips of paper plastered on either side of the doors. In a nearby field, I asked a farmer if anyone lived there. He said two Buddhist nuns and a dozen laywomen had moved into the caves several years earlier. They called their hermitage Laotungmiao, Old Cave Temple.

The Paling area has been attracting people in search of seclusion for at least two thousand years. One such person was Liang Hung, who lived here in the first century A.D. Liang had been herding pigs in the Chungnan foothills when one day his campfire got out of control and burned another man's property. To pay for the damage, Liang gave the landowner his pigs.

Word of Liang's honesty spread throughout the area, and a number of wealthy families offered him their daughters in marriage. Liang declined, saying he preferred to remain single. There was, however, one family whose daughter was unusually fat, ugly, and dark-skinned. She was also strong, so strong that she could lift a millstone. And this last virtue prompted several offers of marriage. But she refused all suitors, saying she would only marry someone as wise as Liang Hung. When Liang heard this, he married her at once and took her to live with him in the hills of Paling, where they supported themselves by farming and weaving. In his spare time, Liang amused himself by playing the zither and composing poems, including a series of twenty-four poems (since lost) about hermits of the past.

Some years later, Liang and his wife got the urge to travel, crossed Heartbreak Bridge, and headed for the central plains. As they passed Peimang, Loyang's famous North Slope Cemetery, Liang wrote this song:

> *climb that north slope oh*
> *look back at the city oh*
> *the palaces soaring oh*
> *the people toiling oh*
> *toiling without end oh*

Another hermit who lived in the hills of Paling was Han K'ang. Han lived here in the second century A.D. and supported himself by gathering herbs and selling them for a set price in Ch'ang-an. He did this for more than thirty years, until one day a young girl stopped to buy herbs from him and became angry when he refused to bargain. She said, "Who do you think you are sticking to one price, Han K'ang?" Han sighed, "I've tried to remain unknown, but now even young girls know my name. What use is it selling herbs?" He went back to Paling and refused to return to the city. But he was not left alone. Having heard of his honesty, Emperor Huan sent an emissary with a carriage and invited him to the capital in Loyang. An imperial summons was difficult to refuse, and Han agreed to go. But while the emissary slept, Han left in his ox cart early the next morning and disappeared into the Chungnan Mountains, where he lived out his years in anonymity.

We followed Han and a thousand other hermits across Pachiao Bridge and three kilometers later passed the bus-stop village of Shaopingtien. The village was named after Shao P'ing, Marquis of Tungling. Tungling (meaning "hills to the east") was the name given to the hills east of the Pa River by the state of Ch'in. When the Ch'in rulers moved their capital to Hsienyang in 362 B.C., they chose this area for their royal graves. As such, it was one of the more important fiefs, and its marquis was chosen with care. A hundred and forty years later, when the state of Ch'in conquered all of China and established the Ch'in dynasty, Hsienyang became the capital of the empire, and Shao P'ing became the Marquis of Tungling. In less than twenty years, the dynasty was over, Hsienyang was in ruins, and Shao P'ing was a commoner. Unruffled by his change of fortune, Shao P'ing turned to growing melons, for which he became even more famous, and melons have remained a specialty of the area. But it was early March, and we kept going.

Four kilometers past Shao P'ing's old melon patch and just before the village of Hsiehkou, we left the main road and turned south. After another four kilometers, just before the village of Hanyu, we took another side road that led southwest. The road was little more than two ruts made by donkey carts carrying bricks from a nearby kiln. After about two kilometers, the road ended at the village of Hungchingpao. On the south side of the village, I found what I was looking for: Kengjuku. Locals called it Kueikou, Ghost Gully.

During the Ch'in dynasty, the First Emperor became annoyed with scholars for presenting conflicting opinions about policies based on different interpretations of the past. His solution was to burn nearly all the books in the empire and to bury 460 scholars alive in a mass grave in 211 B.C. Some modern scholars doubt whether the mass burial actually occurred, but it was reported in the history of the following dynasty and commemorated with a shrine at Kengjuku at least as early as the T'ang and Sung dynasties.

There wasn't much to see. Near the village's former west gate, two huge locust trees marked the site of a shrine that wasn't even a memory among village elders. All they remembered was that some years earlier, a team of historians had come and unearthed a statue of a scholar, which they removed to the Lintung County Museum.

South of the village, wheat sprouts covered a basin a hundred meters wide and five hundred meters long. The villagers said the basin was once a gully that had been filled in. The opinions of modern scholars notwithstanding, I lit some incense. On the way back to the main road, my driver told me that during the Cultural Revolution the Red Guards were fond of reminding intellectuals of the existence of this site.

Back on the highway, we continued east another six kilometers to the county seat of Lintung at the foot of Lishan. Lishan was an isolated spur of the Chungnan Mountains extending about ten kilometers from west to east. It wasn't a very big mountain, and the highest of its two ridges reached only 1,300 meters. But it was conveniently located next to the road that linked the capitals of the Wei River and the Yellow River plains, and it was one of China's first resorts.

I rented a room at the foot of the mountain, and, since the sun was still high, I continued my explorations. Five kilometers east of Lintung, I got out of the car and climbed to the top of the First Emperor's grave mound. It was covered with persimmon trees still waiting for spring. Somewhere down below was the grandest tomb ever built. Its construction was said to have taken seven hundred thousand workers thirty-eight years to complete. Its outer walls had a circumference of over six kilometers. And remains of its various structures, including an underground army of clay soldiers, have been found over an area of fifty square kilometers. Although several exploratory pits have been dug, the mausoleum, into which the emperor was placed in 209 B.C., has remained untouched, too deep for grave robbers.

The mausoleum was a replica of a palace, except that it was cast in copper. Its ceiling was a firmament of pearls. Rivers and lakes flowed with mercury. It was constructed to represent the Taoist paradise the First Emperor sought but never found.

The demands entailed by such construction projects were hardly welcomed by the people whose sweat and blood paid for them. Several years after the First Emperor died, rebellions broke out, and two rebel armies soon defeated the imperial forces. In 207 B.C., their leaders, Hsiang Yu and Liu Pang, agreed to partition the realm.

They met three kilometers north of the First Emperor's underground palace at a place called Hungmen, which was the name of a defile that cut into the loess plateau. Hsiang Yu encamped his forces at the edge of the plateau overlooking the defile, and he invited his rival to a banquet where he planned to assassinate him during a sword dance. One of Liu Pang's advisors, our old friend Chang Liang (Chapter Three), learned of the trap and convinced his lord to act the fool. And when Hsiang Yu saw that Liu Pang was such a weakling, he neglected to give the signal to have him killed. Later, Liu Pang excused himself on the pretext of using the latrine and fled back to his camp at Heartbreak Bridge. He retreated through the Chungnan Mountains but eventually returned, defeated Hsiang Yu, and founded the Han dynasty.

The banquet site has become famous, though few people visit. There's an excellent topographic display of the area in an exhibition hall but little else. When I visited in March, the slope down which Liu Pang escaped was covered by new sprouts of *yin-chen* (*Artemisia capillaris*), a kind of wormwood that people eat in spring to reduce the body's winter heat. My driver gathered enough for a plate of greens, which we shared back at Lishan as part of our own banquet.

The next morning, I began exploring the mountain. As an extension of the Chungnan Mountains, Lishan was home to hermits as far back as records go. But its proximity to the road connecting China's two ancient political centers also led to its early discovery by the elite: there have been villas on the mountain since the eighth century B.C.

Aside from Lishan's convenient location and pleasant scenery, members of the nobility were also attracted by the mountain's hot springs. Winters in north China aren't only cold, they're long. Meteorologists say winter in the Sian area lasts a hundred and forty days, from late October until late March, during which period the average daily temperature remains below ten degrees centigrade (fifty degrees Fahrenheit). To avoid the worst part of the winter, those who could afford it spent the months before the lunar new year soaking in Lishan's open-air, jade-lined baths, which were called "star baths" when they were first built three thousand years ago.

The mountain's main hot spring and most famous bath was located less than one hundred meters east of the hot-spring inn where I spent the night. This was Huaching Pool, frequented by Yang Kuei-fei, the favorite concubine of the T'ang dynasty's Emperor Hsuan-tsung and Lishan's most renowned bather. After her long soaks, she had to be carried out. While she recovered, she would have pollen gathered from an adjacent flower garden and rubbed under her arms to keep herself smelling sweet. Then she would retire to Hsiaoyu Pavilion, to eat persimmons, for which the Lishan area is still famous, or fresh lichees brought from south China by a thousand relay riders.

Behind the steaming, gray-green pools and red-columned pavilions of Huaching Pool, I started up the trail that led to the top of the mountain. After about five hundred meters, I stopped to catch my breath at Tsuchiang Pavilion. This was where Chiang Kai-shek was arrested in 1936. Chiang had come to Sian to ready the Nationalist forces for a final push against the Red Army, which had just reached the end of its Long March in Yenan, 250 kilometers to the north.

Chiang's generals had tried unsuccessfully to dissuade him from continuing his attacks against the Communists; they wanted to form a united front against the invading Japanese Army instead. Several hours before dawn on December 12, Nationalist troops, led by Chiang's own generals, Chang Hsueh-liang and Yang Hu-ch'eng, surrounded the Lishan compound where Chiang was staying. As they approached, one of the soldiers inadvertently fired his rifle, and a gunfight with Chiang's guards ensued.

Alerted by the shots, Chiang slipped out the back window of his room and scaled the compound's rear wall, injuring his back when he fell on the other side. He crawled up the snow-covered slope as far as he could and hid in the crevice above where Tsuchiang Pavilion now stands.

Meanwhile, Chang Hsueh-liang's soldiers shot their way past Chiang's bodyguards and stormed into the generalissimo's bedroom. (It's still there, room 502 in the Wuchienting Guest House, just behind the pool where Yang Kuei-fei once bathed.) The soldiers found no trace of Chiang but noticed that his false teeth were on the bedside table and that his blanket was still warm. Suspecting that Chiang had fled up the mountain, they began searching its slopes and, several hours later, found him hiding in the crevice. Chiang was arrested, taken to Sian, and forced to join the Communists in defending China against the Japanese.

After surveying the scene of Chiang's capture, I climbed up the trail another kilometer to Laochun Temple. In the middle of the eighth century, Emperor Hsuan-tsung built a villa here. And one night while he was staying here, an old man appeared to him in a dream and told him that the semen of the great white star, known in the West as Venus, had fallen to earth and transformed itself into a huge white boulder in the Chungnan Mountains. When the emperor awoke, he sent officials to search for the rock, and when they found it and brought it back, Hsuan-tsung had it carved into a statue of Lao-tzu and placed in a shrine next to his villa.

It was in this shrine that Hsuan-tsung and Yang Kuei-fei knelt side by side one year on the seventh day of the seventh month and vowed to be reborn as the Herdboy Star (Altair in the constellation Aquila) and the Weaving Maid Star (Vega in Lyra). These two stars are said to meet this one night every year on a bridge formed by magpies across the Milky Way. This has been celebrated as Lover's Night in China as long as anyone can remember.

Five years later, when the emperor and his concubine fled from Ch'ang-an during the An Lu-shan Rebellion, the emperor's generals insisted that Yang Kuei-fei be killed before they went any farther. They blamed their difficulties on the emperor's all-consuming romance with her. She was strangled and buried at the side of the road, sixty kilometers west of Sian. Her shrine and grave mound still attract visitors.

While I was looking around the small temple that stands near the spot where she and the emperor knelt, I met Master Su. He was sixty-seven and from Honan. He said he had been a Taoist monk for thirty years and had recently moved to Lishan from Huashan, where he had lived for many years in Yinyang Cave with his teacher, Hsueh T'ai-lai. When I told him I had met Master Hsueh twice in the past year, we became immediate friends and chatted for about an hour. I told him all the Huashan news, and he told me about Lishan. Unfortunately, his dialect was nearly impenetrable, and after sharing a few cups of tea, I got up to leave.

On the way out the front gate, he pointed to two honey locust trees, one male, the other female. He said they were all that remained of the original shrine built by Emperor Hsuan-tsung. The white marble statue of Lao-tzu had been removed some years earlier to the Provincial Museum in Sian, where it has since become one of the most impressive pieces in its impressive collection.

Another kilometer up the mountain's west ridge, I stopped again at Laomutien, a Taoist temple honoring Nu-wa, or Lao-mu, as she's also called, the Mother of Mankind. Nu-wa was the sister and wife of Fu-hsi, who is credited with inventing the eight trigrams that form the basis of the *Book of Changes*. Before she and Fu-hsi were married, she lived alone on Lishan many thousands of years ago. To amuse herself, she mixed water and mud and created the human race. Later, she also saved the world from destruction. After the sky had been seriously damaged during a fight between two gods, she set up a cauldron on Lishan and melted colored rocks to patch the holes. The molten rock left over became the source of the mountain's thermal energy. On the sixth day of the sixth month, people still come to this temple to pay their respects to Lao-mu.

In her shrine hall, I met a young Taoist nun and a young monk. They weren't very talkative and barely looked up from their texts. In the kitchen, another monk was chopping kindling. I introduced myself, and he told me his name was Ch'en Shih-chieh. He turned out to be the abbot. Like his two disciples, he was somewhat suspicious at first. But after we talked for a while, he led me into his room and shut the door. Except for a cot and clothes chest, a table and two stools, the only other objects in the room were a set of keys and his hat (with its hole in the middle for his top-knot) hanging on the wall and half covering the Chinese character for sword. I asked him what Lao-mu, or Nu-wa, had to do with Taoism.

Ch'en: She represents ultimate emptiness. We're all her children, everything is from the womb of her emptiness. It's only through her power that we have heaven and earth, the sun and moon, all things. This is my understanding. It's different from that of other monks. Their understanding comes from books. What I'm telling you is different. Lao-mu and Nu-wa are just names for the nothingness from which time and space and all creation come. Everything comes from nothing. This is Nu-wa. And everything returns to nothing. This is the Tao. This is my understanding.

This is the first time I've ever told this to anyone. No one has ever asked me this question before. I don't like to talk unless there's a reason. I know some Taoist masters have gone to your country to spread Taoism. But their understanding is based on books. All they teach is what's in books. They don't teach the things that come from the spirit. What I'm telling you comes from my own understanding, not from books.

Nowadays, many people have become interested in practicing Taoist meditation and yoga. There are many books that teach this. But what they don't teach is that this isn't the true Tao. In meditation and yoga you go through stages. But the Tao doesn't have any stages. Many people are misled by books, by names, by powers. After they've practiced for a while, they think they've realized the Tao. But they haven't. The Tao has no name. To follow the Tao is to return to nothingness.

People lose the Tao when they try to find it. They confuse existence with nonexistence. All we can do is cultivate *Te* [virtue, spiritual power]. *Te* includes our spirit, our mind, our thoughts. True *Te* leads to true Tao. But what most people cultivate isn't true *Te*. They cultivate powers and thoughts, and they think they've realized the Tao. But they're wrong. To cultivate true *Te* is to get rid of all powers and thoughts, to be like a baby, to see without seeing, to hear without hearing, to know without knowing. First you have to cultivate *Te*. The Tao comes naturally.

But the Tao is empty. It can't be explained. People come here to honor Nu-wa, who represents this emptiness. This isn't superstition. This is part of cultivation. Of course, many people come here to ask Nu-wa for something. This is superstition. But it's not superstition to come here to honor Nu-wa, to remind ourselves to practice the *Te* and Tao of emptiness.

Q: How did you become interested in Taoism?

Ch'en: I had an older brother. He was interested in Taoism. He didn't have a teacher, but he understood Taoist books as soon as he read them. Finally, he saw through the dust of existence, and one day he told me he was leaving home. He didn't tell anyone else. He asked me to take care of our parents and his wife and two children. He said he would leave the next day and never return.

After he left, I took care of our parents until they both died and his children until they were grown. I haven't seen him since he left more than thirty years ago. But before he left, he said if I wanted to find him he would be on one of three mountains. I've already been to two of the mountains looking for him. Next year, I'm going to the third.

When he left, my brother left all his Taoist books behind. At that

Master Ch'en in his room with his hat covering the character for "sword."

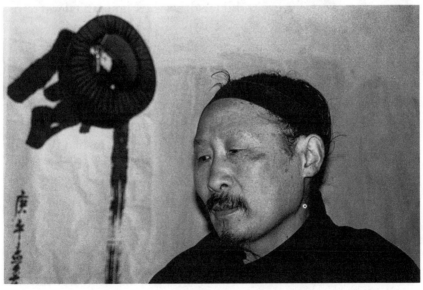

time, I couldn't read. But gradually, I learned. Finally, I became a Taoist monk too. That was only seven years ago. But I've been studying and practicing Taoism ever since my brother left home.

Master Ch'en was an unusally clear-minded, straight-speaking monk, and he had said what he wanted to say and had chores to do. We said good-bye, and I continued up the final slope to the summit of the western ridge. On the summit's northernmost peak was a beacon tower. In ancient times, rulers lit fires on the tower to call the neighboring lords to come to their aid in times of trouble: straw at night, dried wolf dung during the day. And thereon hangs a tale.

During the Chou dynasty, King Yu once offered a thousand gold pieces to anyone who could make his wife, Queen Pao-szu, smile. One official suggested lighting the signal fire to trick all the lords into coming to Lishan. The king agreed, and before long the lords arrived with their soldiers, much to the amusement of King Yu and his wife.

Two years later, in 771 B.C., the Wei River plain was invaded by the nomadic Jung tribe, and King Yu lit the signal fire again. This time, no one came. He was killed at his Lishan villa, and Queen Pao-szu was taken away as a captive. After this incident, the Chou capital was transferred east to Loyang.

I climbed to the top of the tower, which was about ten meters high. But there was too much haze to see very far. I headed back down the mountain. After a few minutes, I turned off on a side trail that led east to the gorge separating the mountain's east and west ridges. Near the bottom of the gorge, I crossed a small bridge and climbed up the opposite slope to what looked like a farmhouse but turned out to be the remains of Shihweng Temple—once considered the most scenic spot on the mountain and famous for its views of the sunsets.

Inside the courtyard, I met two old Buddhist laywomen and a nun so new to her robes she still moved like a young girl. They invited me to stay for tea, and I sat down on a stone stool in the middle of the courtyard. The table was the front side of a Ch'ing dynasty stele that recorded the temple's last renovation and the names of donors.

Although the laywomen taking care of the temple were quite poor, their red earthen teapot was from the great kilns of Yihsing, and their tea was from the famous slopes of Wuyishan. It had none of the delicate fragrance of a fine oolong, but it had the strength of flavor and aroma prized by those who drink tea to clear their eyes and mind prior to meditation. I suggested it tasted like "Bodhidharma's eyelids," and the two laywomen laughed. Legend has it that fifteen hundred years ago, Bodhidharma cut off his eyelids to keep from falling asleep while meditating. Where they fell, the first tea bushes grew.

The older of the women told me she had once been a nun but had been forced to return to lay life by the Red Guards. She married and had a daughter—the young nun, who now leaned against the courtyard wall knitting a cap in the spring sun for winters to come. When the Cultural Revolution ended in the mid-1970s, she returned to Shihweng. She had lived here for the last fifteen years. She said her daughter had shaved her head several weeks earlier in a group ceremony at Big Goose Pagoda in Sian and was waiting to find an appropriate temple at which to live permanently.

After a few cups of tea, we said good-bye, and I retraced my steps to the bridge, then followed the trail down the gorge. Thirty minutes later, the trail ended at the eastern edge of town near the Lintung County Museum. I paid the price of admission and walked inside. In the central hall, I suddenly found myself standing in front of the remains of Shakyamuni Buddha.

After Shakyamuni's cremation twenty-five hundred years ago, the rulers of eight Indian kingdoms were on the verge of going to war over his relics. To avoid bloodshed, they finally agreed to equal shares, which they placed inside stupas in their respective kingdoms. Over the centuries, the contents of these stupas were further divided and redivided, and when the monk Hsuan-tsang returned to Ch'ang-an from India in the seventh century A.D., among the items he brought back were 500 grains of the Buddha's relics.

In 1985, workers digging near a brick kiln about one kilometer northeast of the Hungmen banquet site discovered a stone stupa containing the relics. They had been placed there by Empress Dowager

Wu Tse-t'ien at the end of the seventh century. Several hundred years later, when the dynasty came to an end, the stupa and the temple surrounding it disappeared beneath fields of millet and corn. Since their rediscovery, the relics and the small stupa in which they were found have been placed on display at the Lintung Museum. On the four sides of the stupa are scenes of the Buddha preaching the Dharma and entering nirvana, his disciples burning his body and dividing his relics.

When the body of an ordinary mortal is burned, all that remains are bone chips and ashes. When the body of someone who cultivates a spiritual life is burned, small glasslike or porcelain stones are found. After they reached China, the Buddha's relics were placed inside two glass vials, which were then placed in a small golden casket, which was then placed in an outer casket of silver and mother-of-pearl, which was then placed in the stupa. The relics themselves looked like tiny diamonds. There were several hundred of them.

The stupa, the two caskets, one of the two glass vials and its contents were all in a display case in the middle of the room. While I was taking all this in, the guard had to keep telling people not to spit or smoke. Amidst all the spitting and smoking and shouting, I bowed to the Enlightened One's diamond body and headed back to Heartbreak Bridge. On the way, I recalled a passage in the *Diamond Sutra:*

> "Subhuti, what do you think? Can you see the Buddha's bodily form?"
>
> Subhuti answered, "No, World-Honored One. The Buddha's bodily form cannot be seen. Because the Buddha has taught that bodily form is not bodily form."
>
> Then the Buddha told Subhuti, "Whatever has form is empty. When you see all forms as without form, you see the Buddha."

Chapter Ten

Home
of the
Evening
Star

One hundred and twenty kilometers southwest of Sian is a fifty-four-thousand-hectare expanse of granite and pine known as Taipaishan, a mountain so big even a hundred atomic bombs couldn't wear it down. This, I imagine, is what Chinese military leaders were thinking when they chose it as the perfect place for surviving a nuclear attack. Airmen stationed at Taipaishan are blindfolded and taken on a three-hour jeep ride through a series of switchbacks and tunnels before reaching a network of caverns cut deep inside the mountain. The underground complex was apparently constructed shortly after the Chinese joined the nuclear club and intended as a command center in the event of nuclear war.

Authorities in Sian told me that even with a guide Taipaishan was too dangerous for foreigners to wander around. At the time, I wasn't aware of the danger they had in mind. But even if they had let me go, it wouldn't have been an easy climb. Historical gazetteers say Taipaishan keeps the bones of many who climb it, and Chinese who have hiked to the peak say Taipaishan is more dangerous than Huashan. Hermits, though, have lived on Taipaishan for thousands of years and continue to find seclusion on its slopes. Among the mountain's more

190 □ Road to Heaven

famous recent recluses was Empty Cloud, who moved to Taipaishan in the spring of 1903, following his *samadhi* on Chiawutai, "to avoid the trouble of meeting people." The director of the Shensi Taoist Association told me he knew of two Taoist hermits living on the mountain, and other monks and nuns said they knew of several dozen more.

At 3,767 meters, Taipaishan is the highest of the Chungnan Mountains, and except for several peaks in Taiwan, there's nothing higher east of it in the rest of China. It's one of the few mountains in China that still has large stands of virgin forest. It also has one of the most important and varied collections of flora and fauna in the world. Scientists call Taipaishan the "Botanical Garden of China" and have managed to have the summit and a large section of its western flank declared a nature reserve. Botanists say there aren't any weeds on Taipaishan, only treasures.

Among the 1,700 species of plants found so far on the mountain, more than 600 have medicinal uses. The thuja cedars that hikers first encounter along the mountain's lower slopes are a good example. Their needles are used as an astringent and their seeds as a sedative. As hikers climb to the top, they pass through forests of Huashan pine, chinaberry, birch, fir, and finally, near the peak, stunted blue pine, loquat, and azalea, any of which might be found in an herb collector's backpack.

In addition to its plants, Taipaishan is famous for its animals. Zoologists have spotted 230 species of birds on the mountain, including such rare species as the flightless bustard, the golden pheasant, and the red-crested ibis (the worldwide population of this bird had been reduced to four birds in Japan before several pairs were recently discovered in Taipaishan's foothills). More than 40 species of mammals also make their home on Taipaishan, including the giant panda, the spiral-horned mountain goat, and the golden-haired monkey.

In Sian, I talked with a zoologist who makes yearly trips to the most remote sections of the Chungnan Mountains to collect specimens. In recent years, he's visited several isolated villages near Panfangtzu on Taipaishan's southeastern flank. He said that until now the area's inaccessibility had resulted in a number of hereditary illnesses among villagers, half of whom he judged to be morons or otherwise mentally deficient.

Life on Taipaishan, he said, is dangerous, too. The son of one family in the village of Hupaoku was missing half his face. It had been ripped off by a bear. Another bear had left the boy's father with only one buttock. And the night before the zoologist visited the family, the boy's mother had had to use the bladed end of her carrying stick to kill a leopard near the latrine. The main danger, though, isn't the bears or leopards, it's the wild pigs that travel in herds of up to a hundred, trampling anything and anyone that gets in their way. But despite this danger, village men hunt pigs whenever they can, and village women still use pig bristles to comb and decorate their hair.

The zoologist also told me how villagers guided him and a team of other scientists up Taipaishan to capture a pair of golden-haired monkeys, for which Moscow had offered Peking two trucks and two scholarships. The scientists offered villagers 100 RMB, about twenty dollars, to fill the order. The blue-faced, golden-haired monkeys are still found in loquat forests at higher elevations throughout the Chinling Range. The zoologist described how the villagers first located a band of monkeys near the summit of Taipaishan, crept as close as they could, and then started beating on tin pans. Several of the monkeys simply covered their eyes out of fright and were quickly captured.

The zoologist said that as far as he knew, access to the mountain wasn't restricted, but a guide was absolutely necessary. He suggested I join him on one of his future expeditions or hire a guide in Panfangtzu. I declined both suggestions, preferring to avoid a possible run-in with the mountain's most dangerous species—the Chinese military authorities.

Taipaishan means "great white mountain." But it's had other names. In the third millennium B.C., it was called Tunwu, The Great Provider. And in the second millennium B.C., it was called Tashih-shan, Big Season Mountain. During the first millennium B.C., as early Chinese myth became formalized into philosophy, it was called Taiyi-shan, Mountain of the Great Spirit, creator of all things. Among these creations was its own white granite peak, and by the end of the first millennium B.C., people started calling it Taipaishan.

In early Chinese metaphysics, white was the color of the west and the color of T'ai-pai, the evening star. Over two thousand years ago, the story circulated that the star's semen fell on the mountain and transformed itself into the white rock that made up its summit. (It was apparently this story that was the basis for Emperor Hsuan-tsung's dream in the eighth century A.D.) On rare days when the mountain isn't hidden beneath clouds, its massive white form dominates the view south of Meihsien.

Despite Meihsien's proximity, forty kilometers north of the summit, visitors in ancient times usually came from the east via Wukung or Chouchih, two towns seventy kilometers west of Sian. From Wukung and Chouchih, the traditional route led southwest to the village of Chingchiu, whose ruins are just south of the present town of Huaiya.

Chingchiu was where the original mountain shrine was located, and about ten kilometers south of Chingchiu was the old entrance to the mountain at Sankuan Pond. This was where people came to pray for rain in the seventh lunar month, the only month ordinary mortals dared climb past the foothills. A Ch'ing dynasty official who made the climb left this account of his visit in the *Meihsien Gazetteer*:

> The dangers are unnerving. The trail first follows a stream through a forest but soon becomes a path for birds up a maze of hanging vines, across ravines on fallen trees, along broken ledges. It's like this all the way to the top.
>
> The height is incredible. The ten thousand worries become empty, the sun faint, the moon small, the stars cold, the clouds low. To the southeast, the colors of the sky and mountains are indistinguishable. Past the Wei River to the north, a vast sameness stretches. Mountains like Wuchiang and Chiutsung look like small hills.
>
> The formations are endless. Mountains circle around like stars around the Dipper: slanting, leaning, falling over; arching like an eyebrow, coiling like a dragon, or crouching like a tiger; some are shaped like phoenix wings or ox heads, bear ears or stone bells; some look like Chushan's nine peaks or Chishan's seventy-two pinnacles.

The weather is dramatic. The God of Thunder rumbles in the gorges below, and a rainbow spans the slopes. A sudden whirlwind threatens to blow away a wooden hut, as if it were an autumn leaf. Below, fog locks up the world. Above, the sun looks like it's at the bottom of a well. Then the sky suddenly clears, and all of creation appears.

Another visitor whose impressions are recorded in the *Meihsien Gazetteer* was the seventeenth-century official Chia Li:

When I entered the mountain, I marveled at the strangeness of its scenery: like a Sung or Yuan dynasty landscape, now revealed, now concealed, first this side, then the other, transforming itself into a myriad shapes. And I marveled at the dangers of the trail: like sheep guts or a bird spine, one way up, one way down. Here the world's illusions come to an end.

Ch'en Chung-shun once said, "All anyone needs for climbing mountains is a six-foot staff and a pair of clogs. And yet great lords need to have escorts and provisions before they dare to set off." When I left for Taipai, I couldn't even find a servant to go with me, much less find a staff or clogs to borrow. When I encountered streams and didn't know how deep they were, I threw in rocks or just gritted my teeth and leapt across. The slightest error and I would have perished. When I encountered mud and didn't know how slippery it was, I simply walked across. One misstep and I would have fallen. Peaks that soared like hundred-foot walls, I climbed like an ant going up a tree. Slopes that tilted like thousand-foot roofs, I slithered down like a snake. I had no idea I was so agile or daring.

The detailed account that followed Chia Li's introduction became the standard description of the ascent and was even inscribed in stone for the benefit of future generations. Although I was unable to get anywhere close to the mountain, I learned about its trails from a Taoist monk who had lived on Taipaishan for several decades and who knew all the ways to the top, all four of them: two from the south and two from the north.

The trails from the south include one from the southwest that passes near the nature reserve and another from the southeast that begins along Black River. The trails from the north begin at the villages of Yingtou and Tangyu and converge halfway up the mountain's north side, where they are also joined by the trail from Black River. Most visitors take the two northern trails: Yingtou being the trailhead used by people who come from Meihsien, and Tangyu the trailhead used by people who come from Chouchih. Either way, it's ninety kilometers to the summit for humans and twenty-five for birds.

Also, the trails aren't always open. Even the larger shrines on the mountain are deserted most of the year. In the sixth lunar month, all the monks and nuns in the Taipaishan area meet at the summit. After their meeting, they disperse to the eleven shrines that still dot the trails—before the Cultural Revolution there were thirty-seven.

The monk who told me about Taipaishan said it was a four-day hike to the summit and that few people made the climb except during the height of summer, when the shrines were open and simple food and lodging available. He said most hikers came up between the end of July and the middle of August. Otherwise, it was too cold. Herb collectors and pilgrims, though, were more determined. They could be found on the trails to the summit from April through October collecting plants and the magical water of the mountain's lakes. In his account, Chia Li noted that "people don't linger by these lakes because they harbor strange spirits. If visitors stop too long, the sky explodes with thunder and lightning. It never fails. All the lakes are watched over by spirits, and local people treat them with respect."

In addition to being home to spirits and water-dragons, the lakes hold other mysteries. To begin with, they form a necklace of six cirques around the summit at an elevation of more than 3,500 meters, making them the highest mountain lakes in China and just a breath away from heaven. They were formed twelve thousand years ago during the last ice age. And the largest of them is so deep it's never been fathomed. The monk told me that in 1956 two Soviet divers wearing some sort of underwater breathing apparatus tried to reach the bottom of the biggest lake. After a few minutes, one of them returned to the surface, breathless. The other returned much later, dead. The monk said he looked like a popsicle.

It was Taipaishan's water that prompted Chia Li to begin his account with this note: "Arriving at the mountain, I stabled my horse and went on foot. After walking east for three *li* [two *li* equal one kilometer], I reached Sankuan Pond, the water of which was perfectly transparent. Whoever comes to the mountain to pray for rain needs water for the ceremony. Those unable to climb as far as the peak get their water from this pond." In the eleventh century, when the poet Su Tung-p'o was the magistrate of this area, a drought prompted him to visit the mountain spirit's shrine. Afterward, he wrote this poem:

> *all my life I'd heard of Taipai*
> *I reined in my horse at its sight*
> *let someone beat the drum*
> *see if the rain will come*

Su was referring to another of the mountain's more famous peculiarities. According to the *Shuichingchu*, written in the fourth century A.D., "Armies that travel past Taipaishan shouldn't beat their drums. If they do, wind will arise and rain will fall." When he visited the shrine, Su must have called out the local militia. He said his prayers were answered by a three-day downpour.

Li Pai was another poet the mountain favored. Before Li was born, his mother dreamt she was impregnated by the evening star, and she later gave her son the sobriquet T'ai-pai in honor of his heavenly father. It was only a matter of time before Li Pai, or Li T'ai-pai, visited his rocky half-brother:

> *westward climbing Taipai peak*
> *climbing on in fading light*
> *I heard Taipai say to me*
> *Heaven's Gate will open for you*
> *on I went to ride the wind*
> *and reappeared above the clouds*
> *I can nearly touch the moon*
> *no more mountain underneath*

once you leave Wukung behind
don't plan a quick return

Li Pai was a Taoist, and though Buddhists have also come here to live as hermits, Taipaishan has always been a Taoist mountain. As with other mountains, there are no records of the first hermits who chose Taipaishan as their place of refuge. Taoists say Lao-tzu stopped long enough to collect mica and other ingredients for his elixir before disappearing through nearby Sankuan Pass. But even if Lao-tzu did visit the mountain, he has never been numbered among its recluses.

The first hermit associated with the mountain was Kuei Ku, who lived here in the fourth century B.C. Although Kuei Ku preferred anonymity, two of his students, Su Ch'in and Chang Yi, became famous for initiating a series of political alliances during the Warring States period to establish peace and stability in the region. As a result, Kuei Ku was considered the patriarch of what became known as the Legalist school of eclectic philosophers. Kuei Ku himself was a Taoist and as such is reported to have lived for several hundred years. There's a cliff on Taipaishan named for him. And during the T'ang dynasty, someone produced a Taoist text that bears his name, the *Kueikutzu*.

Considering the mythological basis for the mountain's early names, Taipaishan must have been the scene of religious rituals and spiritual cultivation for several millennia. But the earliest mention of a shrine occurs only two thousand years ago, when one was built in honor of Ku Ch'un in the waning years of the first century B.C.

Ku Ch'un was a minor official at the court of Emperor Ch'eng. He was also a practitioner of Taoist yoga. When he died, his corpse remained warm. And when he was buried, his family refused to nail down the lid of his coffin. Three years later, their son suddenly appeared sitting on top of his village gate. When his family heard the news, they opened his coffin but found only his clothes. After spending three nights on top of the gate and refusing the pleas of his family to return home, he disappeared and later reappeared on top of one of Ch'ang-an's main gates. But again he left after three days. Records say he last appeared on Taipaishan, and afterward someone put up a shrine in his honor at the summit.

The man who became Taipaishan's most famous hermit, however, was another Taoist, Sun Szu-mo. Sun first came here in the early part of the seventh century A.D. and spent much of his life on the mountain collecting herbs, perfecting his knowledge of medicine, and cultivating the Tao. Although several emperors offered him high positions at court, Sun preferred to concentrate on his spiritual and medical practice. He said a doctor must be prepared to treat everyone, regardless of their status or relationship, and he was held in such high esteem by the common people that they called him Yao Wang, the Medicine King. He's still honored as one of China's greatest doctors, as well as its first nutritionist.

When he died, Sun left behind two texts: one summarized medical formulas before his time, and the other included his own extensive contributions, among which were treatments using seaweed and deer thyroid for goiter, ox and sheep liver for nightblindness, and apricots, bran, and peppers for beriberi.

Taipaishan's importance as one of China's major centers of Taoist practice was finally acknowledged in the following century, when the Taoist author Szu-ma Ch'eng-chen listed Taipaishan as the first of the thirty-six Hsiao-tung-t'ien, or Little Caves of Heaven, rectifying its omission among the ten Big Caves—the caves being places where the elixir of immortality could be found or compounded. Li Pai wrote this poem in his *Ku Feng* series around the same time that Taipaishan was added to the list:

> *Taipaishan is every green*
> *encircled above by stars*
> *a hundred miles from court*
> *cut off from the dusty world*
> *here a green-haired ancient*
> *wears a cloud sleeps on snow*
> *doesn't talk doesn't laugh*
> *dwells in silence in a cave*

one day I met this perfect man
bowed and asked his secret
his smile revealed teeth of jade
instructions for elixir
on his bones I read the words
then his form was gone
high above I searched in vain
this endless heat of passion
oh to gather cinnabar sand
to leave mankind forever

Taipaishan wasn't only home to Taoists intent on transforming themselves into immortals, it was also home to Confucian recluses. A recurring theme of China's hermit tradition is that it doesn't represent a renunciation of society so much as a renunciation of greed. As a rule, hermits sought to reform society by first reforming themselves, and many of them came to Taipaishan to cool their passions.

Confucian hermits appeared in Taipaishan's foothills as early as the end of the first century A.D. This was a period that witnessed a great increase in the number of scholars who chose a hermit's hut over a position at court. It was also a time when scholars were interested in extending their customary specialization in one or two of the Confucian classics to a more general education.

Chih Hsun was among the first of these Han dynasty scholars to acquire a profound knowledge of most major texts, and he attracted more than a dozen students to his retreat on Taipaishan. Among them was Ma Jung, whose brilliance soon made him Chih's favorite student. Ma eventually married Chih's daughter and set up his own academy on Taipaishan. By the time he died in A.D. 166, Ma was acknowledged as the dean of commentators on Confucian as well as Taoist classics, and those who claimed him as their teacher numbered more than a thousand.

Among those who came to Taipaishan to study with Ma Jung was Cheng Hsuan. Although he had already studied with many eminent teachers of his time, Cheng was not immediately accepted by Ma. He was forced to build a hut nearby and to receive instruction indirectly through Ma's other students. Once, when Ma was having trouble solving a problem involving the movement of celestial bodies, one of his students said Cheng Hsuan could provide a solution. Cheng promptly obliged and was at last admitted to Ma's inner circle. After studying with Ma Jung for a number of years, Cheng Hsuan left to start his own academy in Ch'ang-an, where he eventually outshone his teacher as a commentator on the classics. As he prepared to leave, Ma grabbed Cheng's hand and said, "The Tao is going east with you. Do everything you can for it."

Whatever he did, it wasn't enough. The Confucian interpretation of the world and man's place in it was soon overwhelmed by Taoism and Buddhism. But when Confucianism finally regained its preeminent position nearly a thousand years later, Taipaishan was once more one of its centers. One of the greatest philosophers of this period was Chang Tsai. Chang was born in Meihsien, just north of Taipaishan, and he retired to its foothills, as Chih, Ma, and Cheng had done in the Han dynasty, to found one of the most famous academies of the Sung dynasty. In the shadow of the Great White Mountain, Chang developed Confucianism's first great metaphysical system based on the theory that our world of objects is nothing more than transient concentrations of *ch'i*, or empty energy, that form and re-form in endless variations. In keeping with his role as a Confucian recluse, he also applied this theory to human relations: we are all made of the same *ch'i* and should treat others as we do ourselves.

On Taipaishan, we see one of the major contradictions apparent in the hermit tradition, and its resolution. Those who follow the Tao cannot divorce themselves from others, yet to find the Tao they must retire from society, at least temporarily, to practice self-cultivation and concentration of mind. If this was true for scholars, it was even more so for monks and nuns, many of whom were inspired in their search for the Tao by living in the home of the evening star, the concentration of the purest *ch'i* in China.

Chapter Eleven

Visiting Wang Wei, Finding Him Gone

*I*n ancient China, choosing a life of seclusion didn't always mean a life of hardship. In addition to religious ascetics and righteous paupers, there were also well-to-do recluses whose aesthetic sensibilities led them out of the city and into the foothills of nearby mountains. Living within a day's journey of Ch'ang-an, impoverished hermits in the Chungnan Mountains occasionally found themselves sharing their huts with the most educated men in China, men who also turned to the mountains for tranquillity and solace.

Despite the pleasures and honors offered to those who followed the road of worldly success, there were always those who turned away: aristocrats tired of court life, would-be officials unable to pass the exams, scholars unwilling to compromise their principles, exhausted bureaucrats, exiled ministers, men one step ahead of the executioner. In every dynasty, the dwellings of educated recluses could be found scattered throughout the countryside, where their occupants spent their days learning to forget.

Sometimes these genteel recluses brought as much luxury to their country homes as they had previously enjoyed in the city. But usually they preferred — or were forced — to leave it all behind and to pursue the joys of a simpler life. Such men have lived in the hills of China for thousands of years. Though their stays in the countryside varied from brief visits to lifelong sojourns, their presence became especially noticeable during periods of prosperity or decline.

In *The Great Age of Chinese Poetry: The High T'ang* (New Haven: Yale University Press, 1981), Stephen Owen notes that "in the eighth century there began in earnest a peculiarly intense relationship between the high official and the recluse or eccentric, a relationship that was to continue in many forms throughout the remaining centuries of traditional Chinese civilization" (p. 27). Actually, the relationship was already ancient by that time. But the eighth century did witness a new twist to the relationship, namely the conscious use of retirement in the countryside as a means of social advancement. This method for gaining the notice of the court and thus securing an official appointment became so prevalent in the T'ang that it became known as the "Chungnan shortcut." During the eighth century, the Chungnan Mountains probably had more huts and villas than at any time before or since. It seems like everybody who was anybody, and anybody who wanted to be somebody, had a Chungnan country home.

Among the genteel recluses living in the Chungnan Mountains, one person who wasn't looking for a shortcut to the capital was Wang Wei. Wang Wei chose the Chungnan Mountains as a shortcut out of town, not into it. It was here, in the relative seclusion of his Wang River hermitage, that he blended life and art in such an overpowering manner that he created a standard to which educated Chinese have been attracted ever since. Wang Wei was the genteel recluse without peer. He took his seclusion seriously, turning seclusion into art and art into seclusion.

Wang Wei was born in A.D. 699 just south of Taiyuan, the capital of what is now the northern Chinese province of Shansi, into two of the most prominent clans in the empire, and his childhood was spent preparing for a career appropriate to his background. The T'ang dynastic history says he began writing poetry at the age of nine. When he died in 761 at the age of sixty-two, Wang Wei was acknowledged by Emperor Tai-tsung as the greatest poet of the age—and no age in

Chinese history witnessed a greater efflorescence of poetic art. Li Pai died the year after Wang Wei at the age of sixty-one, and Tu Fu died eight years later at the age of fifty-eight.

In the centuries since his death, Wang Wei's poetic reputation hasn't dimmed, though he is no longer ranked ahead of Li Pai and Tu Fu. This is hardly a slight. Wang Wei didn't see himself as a poet but as an artist, and as an artist he had no peer. Poetry was only one of several arts in which he excelled. He was also skilled in music, and stories about his ability abound: on one occasion a flute that was unable to bear the strain of accompanying his lute cracked; on another occasion he was shown a mural of an orchestra and was able to tell what note of what song was being played. In fact, after earning the empire's highest academic degree at the unusually young age of twenty-one, he received his first appointment as an official to the imperial court's Music Bureau. But his artistry in music was no match for his poetry, and his poetry was no match for his painting. He tells us:

> *I erred this life writing verse*
> *last life I must have painted*

He was nineteen when he resumed the love of his former life. Though Wang Wei's paintings haven't survived, a number of early copies provide sufficient evidence of his abilities. The Sung dynasty poet Su Tung-p'o called him "China's only truly great landscape artist." And the Ming dynasty calligrapher Tung Ch'i-ch'ang summed up the assessment of his colleagues: "Artists before Wang Wei's time didn't lack skill, but they couldn't transmit the spirit of a landscape. They were hindered by the dust of their senses."

In Ch'ang-an, Wang Wei painted the portraits of such poet friends as Meng Hao-jan and such ancient Buddhist worthies as Vimalakirti, whose name he used as his pen name. But he tired of life at court, especially after several periods of exile for political blunders, first to Shantung and later to the northwest border. Sometime after his fortieth birthday, he bought the former country home of the early T'ang poet Sung Chih-wen. It was located sixty kilometers southeast of

Detail of a painting of a hermit and visitors near his country home, attributed to Wang Wei. Collection of the National Palace Museum, Taipei, Taiwan, Republic of China.

Ch'ang-an along the Wang River. Over the next two decades, he often returned to the capital to maintain the appearance that he was serving in office, and he eventually reached the rank of deputy prime minister. But he spent more and more time at his country home devoting himself to landscape painting and poetry. Among the friends who often joined him was P'ei Ti, with whom he coauthored a series of poems on the sights near his retreat to accompany his famous painting, the *Wang River Scroll*.

As he approached old age, Wang Wei's interest in Buddhism increasingly dominated his life. He spent much of his time in meditation, and his contemporaries say he came to resemble one of the bag-of-bones recluses he once painted. Long before he died, he seems to have already disappeared into one of his paintings or poems.

> *in my prime I loved the Way*
> *a Chungnan cottage in old age*
> *when I want I roam alone*
> *wonders wasted all on me*
> *hiking to the river's source*
> *sitting watching clouds arise*
> *sometimes with an old recluse*
> *talking laughing free from time*

I read Wang Wei's poems soon after coming to Taiwan. I memorized them on my daily hikes into the hills behind the Buddhist temple where I lived for two years. I liked the mood they evoked, and after memorizing one, I would sit and meditate on a grave mound that looked out over the rim of a hill and across the floating city of Taipei. One day as I began to uncross my legs, I noticed a banded krait, one of the world's deadliest snakes, curled up beside me. I got up very slowly—and I didn't memorize any more Wang Wei poems for the rest of my stay at the monastery. Still, my interest in the man remained. And when Steve and I traveled to China fifteen years later to look for hermits, I remembered Wang Wei.

A book I had bought in Hong Kong said that a gingko tree Wang

View of Wang Wei's former estate with present-day facilities visible in the foreground.

Wei had planted was still flourishing on the site of his old hermitage. And one rainy day, with nothing better to do, we decided to pay his tree a visit. We hired a car and took the road southeast along the Pa River. After fifty kilometers, we turned south at Lantien and followed the Wang River through an opening in the Chungnan Mountains. When Wang Wei visited his country home, he had to dismount here and go the rest of the way by boat. There was no path, much less road, until the government blasted one along the gorge's eastern edge in the 1950s.

Halfway through, a landslide blocked our way. Workers said they expected to have it cleared in a few days. Clambering over the slide, I stopped to look at some blue daisies that turned out to be old friends. Along the paths near my home in Taiwan, my wife often picked their leaves for dinner. I was surprised to see them so far north. On the other side of the slide, Steve and I joined half a dozen locals aboard a motorized three-wheeler.

As we left our car and the landslide behind, the gorge soon gave way to a broad valley surrounded on all sides by misty green peaks. The other passengers got out at the villages of Yentsun and Kuanshang. To the east of Kuanshang I looked for Mengchengao, the site of Sung Chih-wen's original retreat and the place where Wang Wei lived when he first came here and where his series of poems on the Wang River began. But the site was now the home of Wang River High School. We continued heading southeast.

Past the village of Paiyaping, the road forked right to Wang Wei's gingko and his former Deer Park retreat, another kilometer or so away. The driver suggested we go left instead and first visit a cave from which we would have a good view of the area.

We passed some kind of checkpoint. But it was raining, and whoever was on duty must have been inside. A few minutes later, I noticed a police car following far behind. We kept going. The road turned to mud, mud turned to rocks. When the rocks turned to boulders, we got out and climbed.

After a few minutes, we reached a terrace that overlooked the surrounding mountains. A caretaker appeared from a small shed and unlocked the gate to Lingyun Cave, which included the usual stalactites and stalagmites shaped like Kuan-yin, Bodhisattva of Compassion. We preferred the view outside, and we stood on the terrace watching the peaks disappear and reappear, as if one of Wang Wei's scrolls were being unrolled before us, one scene at a time.

When the mist turned to heavy rain, we headed back down. Through a break in the clouds, I noticed several policemen standing around our three-wheeler. I told Steve to change film and put the exposed roll in his sock. When we reached the road, the police informed us that we were under arrest and escorted us back to the landslide. There we were met by another police car and taken, siren blaring all the way, to the Foreign Affairs Police Headquarters in Sian, where we were accused of spying. Though we hadn't gotten that far, the gingko tree planted by Wang Wei at his Deer Park retreat turned out to be in the middle of a nuclear weapons factory. Apparently Tu Fu had a similar experience:

> *visiting Censor Wang's retreat*
> *why the silent pines bamboos*
> *bramble gate closed and locked*

Chapter Twelve

When the
Tao Comes
to Town

*I*n the *Lankavatara Sutra,* the Buddha says, "Compassion comes from wisdom." For the past five thousand years, individuals in China searching for wisdom, whether they called it the Dharma or the Tao, have invariably looked for it, and sometimes found it, in the mountains. But sooner or later, wisdom gives rise to compassion. Sooner or later, the Tao comes to town.

Buddhists who brought the Tao to town were called *p'u-sa,* or bodhisattvas. Taoists were called *hsien,* or immortals. By their own admission, few Taoists got that far. But some did, though they were always hard to find — for those who did lived apart from others. If they didn't leave the world altogether and fly off to the Islands of the Blessed, they usually lived in mountains, deserts, and marshlands. But they also frequented the temples, marketplaces, and wineshops of civilization: they came to town to find someone to teach.

In Ch'ang-an, or Sian, the meeting place for visiting immortals for the last thousand years has been Pahsienkung, the Temple of the Eight Immortals. It was built in the eleventh century on the site of an earlier Taoist shrine and next to the wineshop where Lu Tung-pin met the immortal Han Chung-li in the eighth century.

呂先生

鍾離處士

江山道人劉志順刊

長安慶雲觀王守真 立石

Rubbing of Lu Tung-pin and Han Chung-li from a stele at Loukuantai.

Lu and Han were the founding members of a group of recluses that by the thirteenth century were known as the Eight Immortals. Several hundred years earlier, the poets Li Pai and Tu Fu were included as members of the Eight Immortals of Wine, and references to a group of eight sages go back much earlier. But none of these earlier groups elicited the same amount of patronage, much less veneration, as Lu and Han's group. Of course, Taoism recognizes hundreds if not thousands of immortals, just as Buddhism recognizes hundreds if not thousands of bodhisattvas. Why these eight were chosen for special attention is unclear. And who was responsible for their selection is also unknown. Besides their Taoist cultivation, the only other thing they had in common was that most of them cultivated the Tao in the Chungnan Mountains.

Though the members of the group have changed from time to time, the choice of eight was apparently an attempt to give the eight trigrams in the *Book of Changes* human form. As such, the eight immortals are said to represent various sets of yin-yang relationships, such as first and last, old and young, male and female, beautiful and ugly.

The first of the eight is Han Chung-li, who is often portrayed holding a fan with his belly bared to the wind. As his name suggests, he was born during the Han dynasty, in the first century A.D. He was a general and was sent to fight the Tibetans, who had been raiding the Wei River plain west of the capital. When he was defeated, he fled in disgrace into the nearby Chungnan Mountains, where he met several Taoist masters, who imparted to him the secrets of immortality. Eight hundred years later, he passed on these secrets to Lu Tung-pin, including instruction in a series of eight exercises that are still practiced for promoting the circulation of *ch'i*.

The last of the eight immortals is Ts'ao Kuo-chiu, who usually holds a pair of imperial emblems. He was the younger brother of Empress Ts'ao of the Sung dynasty, whose husband is said to have given Ts'ao the two emblems to assure him of universal hospitality and respect. One day Han Chung-li and Lu Tung-pin found Ts'ao meditating in the Chungnan Mountains. When they asked him what he was cultivating, Ts'ao said he was cultivating the Tao. When they asked him the location of the Tao, Ts'ao pointed to heaven. And when they asked the location of heaven, he pointed to his heart. The two immortals laughed, congratulated Ts'ao on his understanding of the Way, and asked him to join them.

The eldest member of the group is Chang Kuo Lao, Old Chang Kuo, who carries a bamboo tube called a *yu-ku,* or fish-drum, and who rides a white donkey, usually backwards. The donkey can travel a thousand miles in a single day. It can also be folded up like a piece of paper and later brought back to life by spraying water on it. Although his biographies in both T'ang dynastic histories say he was born in the eighth century, Chang is also said to have been a white bat at the beginning of creation and thus is considered the group's senior member.

The youngest member is Han Hsiang-tzu, nephew of the ninth-century scholar and poet Han Yu. Usually portrayed playing a flute, he was criticized by his uncle for not preparing for a career as an official. In response, Han Hsiang-tzu wrote a poem describing the joys of his solitary life in the Chungnan Mountains living on dew, rose-colored clouds, and ground-up pearls. But it wasn't until he demonstrated his power to make peonies bloom in winter that he finally convinced his uncle he was meant to follow the Tao and not the imperial retinue.

Lu Tung-pin is by far the most popular of the eight immortals and has become the patron saint of several arts and crafts, including literature. Representing masculinity, he is usually shown with a sword slung over his back and a fly whisk in his hand. The sword renders him invisible and allows him to cut through troubles. The fly whisk indicates authority and the status of a teacher.

During a chance meeting with Han Chung-li in a Ch'ang-an wineshop in the eighth century, Lu fell asleep and saw himself pass through a life of worldly successes and failures, joys and griefs. (His dream has been immortalized in a thirteenth-century play known as *The Yellow Millet Dream.*) When he awoke, he asked Han how to overcome life's transience. Han instructed him in Taoist cultivation, and Lu went to live as a recluse, first in the Chungnan Mountains and later in the Chungtiao Mountains, eventually becoming an immortal himself. In addition to instructing other members of this distinguished group, Lu left behind several treatises, one of which has been translated into English under the title *Secret of the Golden Flower*. He also wrote simple poems to enlighten others, several dozen of which were collected in the *Chuantangshih* (Complete Poems of the T'ang):

> *I have pine wind for sale*
> *have you ever tried it*
> *three tons of gold*
> *gets you a gourdful*

The only female member of the group is Ho Hsien-ku, who holds a lotus leaf or sometimes a magic mushroom. Coming from the Canton area, she was also the only southerner in the group. She refused to marry and wandered alone in the mountains, gathering wild fruits and plants to support her mother. Eventually, she stopped going anywhere near the smoke and dust of civilization and learned to survive on a diet of mica, which made her so light she was able to whisk through the mountains like a bird. One day, she met Lu Tung-pin and received from him the peach of immortality.

Lan Ts'ai-ho is the handsomest member of the group and is sometimes portrayed as a girl. His biography first appeared in the Sung dynasty, which suggests that he was born somewhat earlier, probably in the ninth or tenth century. He wanders around selling flowers, singing songs about immortality to the accompaniment of two long wooden clappers, wears only one shoe, and is dressed in clothes forever unsuited to the season.

Finally, the ugliest of the eight immortals is Li T'ieh-kuai, Iron Crutch Li. While living in the Chungnan Mountains, Li learned how to leave his body for days at a time. After one such trip he returned to find that it had been burned by his disciple, who had taken his master for dead. Fortunately, he was able to find the body of a lame beggar who had just died and was able to use it as his own. Ever since then, he has hobbled around on an iron crutch.

The day before we were detained by the police, Steve and I had visited the temple where these eight immortals once met, and perhaps still meet. It was at its original location, about five hundred meters northeast of Sian's East Gate. The temple, though, has seen better days. A factory that had taken up the entire main courtyard was only recently dismantled. The government has apparently decided the temple has tourist potential and has funded a certain amount of renovation. At the rear of the grounds, we visited the recently restored shrines honoring the Eight Immortals and the Lady of the Southern Dipper.

At one of the renovated shrines, Steve and I joined other visitors in lighting incense, making wishes, and choosing bamboo sticks with numbers on them. I chose number two and went to a nearby window, where I paid the equivalent of five cents for my fortune. It began, "Those who are hidden one day shine forth."

I walked over to a group of Taoist monks. One of them turned out to be the abbot. I told him I was looking for hermits. He said my fortune promised success. Steve and I had visited the Taoist temples on Wutangshan in Hupei Province several months earlier and had heard about six-hundred-year-old Taoist masters living deep in the Shennungchia Mountains. I asked the abbot if there were any masters that old living in the Chungnan Mountains. He said he had heard similar reports from herb collectors but had never met anyone older than 150. He asked me how old Steve was.

Everyone we met in China wanted to know how old Steve was. One look at his beard convinced them he must be ancient. I smiled and said Steve was 500 and that he had come to China to find someone older. This sent shock waves through the temple and soon every Taoist in the place was gathered around. I tried to undo the damage and told them that I was only joking, that Steve was a whisker under fifty. It was like puncturing a balloon. You don't joke with Taoists about old age.

A week later, we found ourselves back at Pahsienkung. After letting us turn in the wind for three days, the foreign affairs police had finally decided we were too dumb to be spies. As they handed back our passports, they warned us that conducting interviews was grounds for deportation. They were somewhat concerned that the purpose of our trip was to talk with people over whom they had no control, no matter that they were harmless hermits.

I looked over my shoulder as we reentered Pahsienkung. No one looked suspicious enough to warrant our turning back. Usually Steve and I attracted a crowd wherever we went, but this time as we walked through the courtyard, it was as if we had become invisible. An intermediary had arranged for me to interview one of the temple's resident monks. We arrived at Master Yang's room on the east wing completely unobserved. I knocked, and a voice said to come in. We went in, and I closed the door to make sure we wouldn't be disturbed.

Master Yang had been meditating, and he didn't bother to uncross his legs. At one end of the bed on which he was sitting was a mosquito net. Next to the other end was the bed of his disciple, who was away for the day. The only other furnishings included two wooden trunks for clothes and possessions, two wooden desks, and two folding chairs. I sat down on one of the chairs and asked Master Yang how old he was. He said he was only seventy-two, not very old at all. He said he had been a monk for nearly fifty years. I asked him about cultivating the Tao.

Yang: Cultivating the Tao is like being a fetus. When we're inside our mother, we can't see or hear a thing. All we know is our own feelings. We don't know we're inside our mother or who she is. When we can see and hear, then we're born. Cultivating the Tao is the same. When we finally know the Tao, our cultivation is over. But first we have to spend a long time cultivating. What we cultivate, though, isn't this physical body. Lao-tzu didn't talk about this body. Our physical body isn't our true body. Our true body is inside our false body, just like the fetus is inside its mother. Our mother is our false body. Our true body doesn't appear until we leave our false body behind.

Q: Do people who cultivate the Tao look different?

Yang: Yes and no. A number of years ago I met an old Taoist monk at Loukuantai. His name was also Yang, and he only ate one meal a day, which was unusual. At that time there were more than a hundred Taoists living at Loukuantai, and he was the only one who ate just one meal a day. Other than his morning meal, he didn't have a schedule. He slept whenever he felt like it. And when he wasn't sleeping, he worked. He had more spirit and energy than the others, but other than that he didn't seem special. A few years later there were some changes at Loukuantai, a dispute about leadership, and he was asked to take over as abbot. I saw him again a year or so later when he came to Pahsienkung for a meeting. He was completely different. His eyes looked different. His voice sounded different. Suddenly he acted like someone who cultivated the Tao. But he hadn't revealed this side of himself before, because his responsibilities had been different then.

Q: Why did you decide to devote yourself to the Tao?

Yang: The reason I left home and became a monk was to study. When I grew up, I didn't have the chance to go to school. My family was too poor. My cousins, though, went to school, when they weren't busy with farm work. But my father said it hadn't done them any good. Still, I wanted to learn something. And when I was almost twenty, my older brother agreed to let me go to school. I studied three or four years, but I didn't learn much, just enough to read stories. I didn't really learn to read until I left home and became a monk. Since then, studying has caused me a lot of trouble. It wasn't as easy as I thought. It was like wind blowing past my ears. So I decided I'd better concentrate more on practice than on study. Still, over the years I've read whenever I could.

After Liberation we weren't supposed to read old books anymore. But I managed to collect quite a few Taoist books, and I hid all the important ones away. Then the Cultural Revolution came, and they started burning books and arresting people. By that time I knew what was inside the books. So when the Red Guards came and demanded we hand over our books, I brought out a whole chest of them, including things that I had written. I told them to take what they wanted and leave me the rest. They took everything into the kitchen and burned it.

Q: What a pity. Were you upset?

Yang: Not really. It was just change. Besides, after the Cultural Revolution I was able to collect another chest of books, and I was able to do some reading almost every day. Then about seven years ago I lost my eyesight and gave away all my books.

Q: What happened to your eyes?

Yang: Taoist practice can be dangerous. I did something wrong, and they went out like a couple of candles.

Q: What books on Taoism did you like the most?

Yang: Of course, the *Taoteching*. After Liberation, people criticized the *Taoteching* a lot. But not now. Now they agree it's the most profound book in the Taoist canon. Most Taoist books reveal themselves as deep or shallow as soon as you read them. But not the *Taoteching*. The *Taoteching* is only for people of deep understanding. It's not for ordinary people. It was the first Taoist book. After that came Huang-ti's *Yinfuching,* which is even briefer than the *Taoteching* in explaining the essentials of Taoist philosophy and practice.

But the most important, the most precious of all Taoist books is the Jade Emperor's *Hsinyiching,* which is the most essential part of the *Huangching.* We use it in our morning and evening services. It's the teaching transmitted by the Jade Emperor. It's not about external things. It explains how we're all miniature universes, how we all have the sun, the moon, the stars, and space inside us. It's about how to use our *ch'i* to nourish and protect our mortal body and how to concentrate our *ch'i* to create an immortal body. If our *ch'i* only comes from the outside, we're easily exhausted. It teaches us how to cultivate our inner *ch'i.* Cultivating the Tao isn't easy. Some people cultivate all their lives without success. The key is to concentrate your *ch'i.* Once you concentrate your *ch'i,* your wisdom will arise naturally, as easily as a flame rises and rain falls.

Q: Did you find books useful in learning Taoism?

Yang: Books are like food. They can fill our stomachs but not our minds. If we don't know something, we can buy a book and learn about it. We can learn a lot from books. But after we're finished reading, we discover that what books talk about is different from reality.

Master Yang, the blind Taoist.

There are many books about love now. Some monks read these books and decide to return to lay life, to get married and have children. But love changes and becomes meaningless. Books can deceive. And practice takes time. It's a shame to spend years practicing the Tao and then return to lay life only to be disappointed. It's very hard to begin practicing again.

If you're going to cultivate the Tao, you have to be prepared for hardships. Unless you're born with advantages, you're going to suffer. But from suffering comes joy. It's like with money. If it comes easy, it goes easy. If you have to work for it, money means more. You don't waste it. It's the same with cultivating the Tao. If you're born into a good family and receive a good education, it's easier. If you're not, you need to have greater determination. But understanding the Tao takes a long time, and it takes great determination to succeed. Many people cultivate the Tao, as many as the hairs on an ox. But success takes time. Those who truly cultivate the Tao are very few. And those who succeed are even fewer.

Q: What difference do you see between Buddhism and Taoism in terms of practice?

Yang: Buddhists and Taoists walk the same path. They just dream different dreams. Essentially Buddhism and Taoism are the same. Their sacred texts talk about the same things. It's just that Taoism emphasizes life, and Buddhism emphasizes nature. But people who truly cultivate cultivate both. In terms of actual practice, Buddhism is somewhat better than Taoism. Even though Taoists talk about cultivating the mind, they often have a harder time controlling their emotions. They have a harder time suppressing feelings of pride. But to cultivate either of them successfully is very hard.

Q: Has Taoism changed in recent decades?

Yang: The Tao never changes. What we eat and wear has changed, but the Tao hasn't changed. There have been advances in science and society, but so what? We're eating better now. But it's the same old Lao-tzu.

Q: Can you support yourself by instructing people about Taoist practice?

Yang (laughing): It's like making tofu. When a tofu master decides to teach what took him years to learn, how should he count up what it cost him in charging an apprentice? There's no bill for instruction in the Tao.

There may not have been a bill, but it was time to leave, time to say good-bye to Master Yang and the hermits of the Chungnan Mountains and, for that matter, to China.

My last day in Sian, I went to buy some stamps for my son. The stores specializing in stamps were at the end of Poshulin Road, not far from the city's South Gate. I passed up the Ch'ing dynasty stamps and the Cultural Revolution stamps and bought a bunch of stamps with flowers and famous beauties of the past. Then I headed back up Poshulin Road. I hadn't gone more than a hundred meters, when I noticed a small hand-painted sign on the right: Wolungszu, Temple of the Sleeping Dragon. I'd read about Wolung Temple. This was where Empty Cloud stayed before he moved to Chiawutai at the end of the Ch'ing dynasty. I'd heard that it had been destroyed by the Red Guards, but here was a sign that said otherwise. I followed it into a lane for about fifty meters to a rusty metal gate. Inside was Wolung Temple.

During the T'ang dynasty, it was called Kuanyin Temple, and in the Sung dynasty, its name was changed to Sleeping Dragon in honor of Wei-kuo, an abbot of the temple who practiced meditation in a reclining position.

The metal gate creaked. The front courtyard was deserted. Another factory had recently been dismantled. The temple buildings were old and in such sorry repair, I almost turned back. Past the inner courtyard, I went inside the main shrine hall. After lighting some incense and paying my respects, I noticed a small stone buddha. The attendant told me it had been carved at the end of the fifth century. He also pointed out a T'ang dynasty painting of Kuan-yin. Incredible treasures for such a dilapidated temple.

Just as I was leaving, several monks appeared at the door. When they asked me what I was doing, I told them I was visiting hermits. They laughed. One of them said, "Then you've come to the right place. We're all hermits here." I couldn't help but laugh too. The monk's name was Ju-ch'eng. He was obviously the abbot, though he denied it—he said he was too dumb to be an abbot. Then he explained that Wolung Temple refused to have an official abbot. He said, "If we choose an abbot, he has to be approved by the government. We prefer to be left alone. That's why we don't fix up the temple. The government has offered us money to repair the buildings. But this is a Zen temple. We don't need fancy buildings. Fancy buildings just attract tourists."

He told me there were about fifty monks living at the temple. Two of them, he said, were in their eighties. Their names were Hui-ching and Hui-t'ung. He said they got up every morning at three and didn't go to sleep until shortly before midnight. They spent most of their waking hours on their meditation cushions. I asked Ju-ch'eng who their master had been, but I should have known the answer. He said, "Empty Cloud."

We talked for half an hour about Wolung Temple and about the Chungnan Mountains. The temple, he said, had four seventy-day meditation sessions every year. Then he started listing all the hermits he knew in the mountains. I knew all of them. I smiled and told him this was the first time I had met city hermits. He laughed, and so did I. And then I remembered the Chinese saying: "The small hermit lives on a mountain. The great hermit lives in a town." Having nothing left to say, I bowed and said good-bye.

Huashan.

Note on the Spelling of Chinese Names

The Wade-Giles system is used throughout except for place names, where the hyphens and apostrophes have been removed and the words run together (Kuanyin instead of Kuan-yin, Taipai instead of T'ai-pai), and for names for which a prior usage has been established (Peking instead of Peiching).

Acknowledgments

Work on this book would not have been undertaken or completed without the generous support of

Winston Wang and the Ming-Teh Foundation,
Ven. Chih Chung and the Pei-Kwang Foundation,
Fred Goforth, Dana Morgan, and Bryan Curtis

About the Author
and the Photographer

Bill Porter is a writer and translator. Among his previous publications, under the name of Red Pine, are *The Collected Songs of Cold Mountain*, *The Mountain Poems of Stonehouse*, and *The Zen Teaching of Bodhidharma*. Since 1972 he has lived in Taiwan and Hong Kong and has traveled extensively in China. He is currently working on a book about the Yellow River and on a translation of Sung Po-jen's *Guide to Capturing a Plum Blossom*, the first book of art or poetry ever printed, as well as on translations of a number of ancient Buddhist texts.

Steven R. Johnson is a photographer whose previous published works include *Here among the Sacrificed*, a photographic and written account of riding the freight trains along the West Coast of the United States produced in collaboration with poet Finn Wilcox. Johnson lives in Port Townsend, Washington, and spends part of each year repairing fishing boats at the Port Townsend boatyards.

Cover design: Sharon Smith
Calligrapher: Fu Sheng Fu
Text art director: Sharon Smith
Text design: Zipporah Collins
Compositor: Stanton Publication Services
Editor: Thomas Christensen
Production coordinator: Hazel White
Copyeditor: Alice Klein
Proofreaders: Karen Stough and Mu'frida Bell
Cartographer: Bill Nelson
Printer and binder: Data Reproductions Corporation